UPTON-*Upon* SEVERN Recollections

Margaret Bramford

MALCHIK MEDIA

A Malchik Media & richardlynttonbooks Publication

Published by
Malchik Media & richardlynttonbooks

Copyright © 2022 Richard C.G. Lyntton

ISBNs:
979-8-9860794-6-2 Paperback
979-8-9860794-8-6 Hardback
979-8-9860794-5-5 eBook

Library of Congress Control Number: 2022909930

Cover and interior repackaging by Gary A. Rosenberg ~
www.thebookcouple.com

About the cover image:

Florence Bramford (circled), lifelong Upton-upon-Severn resident and book contributor, poses for royal household group photo with The Queen Mother during a Royal Tour in East Africa circa 1948.

Thank you in advance for reading
Upton-Upon-Severn Recollections:
Worcestershire & Malvern
History Series Book 3

• • • • • • • • • • • • • • • •

You might also enjoy *From Cottage to Palace ~*
Worcestershire & Malvern History Series Book 1
https://www.amazon.com/dp/B09WB2LQHM
Listen now on Audible at:
https://www.audible.com/pd/From-Cottage-
to-Palace-Audiobook/B0B3PQTSGZ
and
This Was OUR MALVERN, Volume 1
https://www.amazon.com/gp/product/B0B1JHQSJH

For more information about the Worcestershire
& Malvern History Series by Margaret Bramford,
or to sign up for our FREE richardlynttonbooks
(fiction and nonfiction) newsletter, VISIT
this richardlynttonbooks website link:

https://richardlynttonbooks.com/contact/

If you enjoyed the book, we would very much
appreciate it if you could leave a review on
the platform you used. Thank you so much!

Contents

● ● ● ● ● ● ● ● ●

The Morris Family of Severn Stoke in 1913.
Top row from left: Mary, Jack, May, Fred. Second from
left: Doris, Stanley, William (father), Jane (mother) with
Kath, Chris, Louisa. Sitting on grass: Edith, Joan, Bill

Acknowledgements

. . . .

This book is a light-hearted Social History of a riverside town in Worcestershire. These are the memories of Upton-upon-Severn dwellers, spanning mainly the first half of the twentieth century. The author dedicates this book, with gratitude, to the people who shared their memories with her. Margaret has preserved their lively speech and their cheerful outlook on life.

Contributors
(in alphabetical order)

Doreen Beach (née Biddle)

Avril Bramford

Florence Bramford

Edith Chescoe

Cathie Guilding
(née Galley)

Austin Hartwright

Jack Hayfield

Kath Hill (née Morris)

Enid Loynes

Patrick Nance

Lavinia Nind

Joan Preece (née Walton)

Doll Smith

Elsie Trapp (née Hicks)

Jim Trevor

I thank the following for the loan of photographs:
John Talbot Cooper
Kath Hill
Malvern Gazette & Ledbury Reporter

We dedicate this book to Her Majesty Queen Elizabeth II
(1926 to 2022)

With gratitude for a job well done and second to none!

The following message is from then Princess Elizabeth's 21st birthday speech, broadcast around the world from South Africa in 1947.

Let me begin by saying thank-you to all the thousands of kind people who have sent me messages of good will. This is a happy day for me, but it is also one that brings serious thoughts—thoughts of life looming ahead with all its challenges and with all its opportunity. Will you, the youth of the British family of nations, let me speak on my birthday as your representative? Now that we are coming to manhood and womanhood, it is surely a great joy to us all to think that we shall be able to take some of the burden off the shoulders of our elders who have fought and worked and suffered to protect our childhood. If we all go forward together, with an unwavering faith, a high courage, and a quiet heart, we shall be able to make of this ancient commonwealth, which we all love so dearly, an even grander thing. More free, more prosperous, more happy, and a more powerful influence for good in the world than it has been in the greatest days of our forefathers.

To accomplish that, we must give nothing less than the whole of ourselves. There is a motto which has been born by many of my ancestors, a noble motto: 'I serve.'

Those words were an inspiration to many bygone heirs to the throne when they made their nightly dedication as they came to manhood. I cannot quite do as they did. But through the inventions of sounds, I can do what was not possible for any of them. I can make my solemn act of dedication with the whole empire listening. I should like to make that dedication now. It is very simple:

> 'I declare before you all that my whole life whether it be long or short shall be devoted to your service and to the service of our great imperial family to which we all belong.
>
> But I shall not have strength to carry out this resolution alone unless you join in it with me as I now invite you to do. I know that your support will be unfailingly given. God help me to make good my vow and God bless all of you who are willing to share in it.'

1 ~ The Bramfords of Bramford Cottage

● ●

"This little maid is my granddaughter." The tall, slim, silver-haired man who spoke these words to the saw-mill owner at Longden Heath, looked proudly down at me. I was six, warmly clad in a 'Red Riding Hood' style red cloak and hood.

"Keep close by me," warned my Grandad. "Don't go near the machine."

Workmen were feeding this noisy monster with tree trunks to make fences.

We had walked from his ancient cottage up the road, next door to the Rose and Crown Inn. He and Grandma had lived there for 41 years since their marriage in 1888. We children were familiar with the Elizabethan bedrooms' old oak beams, hand-cut, with their original pieces of bark still attached.

Staying with Grandma meant sleeping on soft, goose-feather mattresses. We washed from a china jug and basin on the washstand, aided by a brown metal can of hot water, brought upstairs by an aunt. We always used green Palmolive soap at Grandma's. It was all very different from home. The cottage had a baker's oven from long ago.

Going down the steep staircase for breakfast, we would be greeted by the smell of porridge and bacon cooking. And through the stout kitchen door, from the sunlit garden crept the spicy aroma from the two-foot-high box hedges, which surrounded the large, well-tended vegetable plots. It was a welcoming and reassuring home.

But the smell from the outside loo, an earth closet, was not so attractive. It was partly disguised by the frequent use of Jeyes powder or strong carbolic. I did not like the disinfectant odour of stiff Izal toilet paper either. And the coloured text nailed to the wall proclaimed, 'Jesus wept'.

In our lovely School House at Overbury, we were used to a flushing toilet, and water on tap from the springs on Bredon Hill. Here, at the cottage, they depended on a pump in the garden for all their water. But it never ran dry and the water had an earthy taste. Bath night for Grandma's children had been in an old tin bath, now hanging on an outside wall.

Grandad had come to Worcestershire in about 1880, aged 18. His home until then had been the mediaeval village of Laxton in Nottinghamshire, where the Open Field system still operated. Son of a farmer, Grandad George Bramford had been recommended by the Reverend Henry Martin of Laxton, to be a groom in the household of his brother-in-law, Colonel Sir Charles Johnson, of The Hill, Upton-on-Severn.

With his upright, spare figure, clean-cut features, and alert and steady gaze, George Bramford became a reliable coachman. However, at the turn of the 20th century, when cars had been invented, he became a chauffeur, and thereafter remained in the service of the Johnson family for the rest of his working life. In the early 1880s, a new young Lady's Maid had arrived at The Hill. She was petite and lively, with dark hair and twinkling brown eyes. She was to become my grandmother.

Eva Alice Wills had come from Somerset, recommended by another branch of the Martin family living in Devon. She had been appointed to be Lady's Maid to the two step-sisters of Lady Jemima Johnson. Their names were Miss Charlotte and Miss Renira Martin.

One of Eva's duties was to warn coachman George when to be ready with her Ladies' carriage. He found her attractive, and they became engaged. Norman May of Malvern took their engagement photos. Eva wears a dark velvet bustled dress, a brooch, and a locket. George wears a cut-away coat and waistcoat. His tiepin is a gold horseshoe.

They were married in Eva's hometown of Bridgwater, Somerset, in 1888. Their Newbridge Green cottage had previously housed a Dame School for local children, kept by Mrs. Cowley. As a young man, George Bramford had been her lodger.

Edith Chescoe, as a child living near the cottage, remembered my Grandad. "He was a very tall man. He wore those lovely big boots and leather leggings, always polished up, 'cos he was groom to Colonel Johnson. As a little girl, I would walk up from our cottage to Bramford's corner. He would be cutting the hedge of the cottage by the road. And that hedge was six feet tall. He would have a ladder to climb up.

And he drove the pony and trap. The Johnsons were one of the first in Upton to buy a car and your Grandad became their chauffeur."

Austin Hartwright recalled the car driven by George Bramford. "When I left Upton School, aged 14, I worked for Lady Johnson. Colonel Johnson had died by then. One of my jobs was to help your Grandad clean the car for the Lady to go out in. It was kept in the coach-house, 'cos the horses weren't there anymore. A smashing car it was! A Daimler, I believe. A beautiful car.

Your Grandad had to go to Birmingham to learn how to

drive it. He would stand at the top of the long drive, with the car all polished ready for the Lady's outing. He would be wearing his smart navy blue uniform. The parlour maid would wave for him to drive to the front door, ready to go.

It was very rare in the early 1900s to see a car on the road. Chauffeurs would drive at 30-40 m.p.h.—faster than a horse and carriage. Lady Johnson's car was a real smart one. I remember the fresh smell of leather inside. It had real leather upholstery, which felt like velvet. It always looked new. But I never had a ride in it!"

Austin told me further memories of my Grandparents. "Your Grandad had a big old-fashioned garden, with pigs and poultry. I got on fine with him. There was nothing blusterous about him. He'd got a rare old laugh, occasionally.

Your Grandma? She was sweet. In looks, you remind me slightly of her—the shape of the face and the features. At the cottage, I would get a cup of tea. She was a real nice person. I used to get on well with her too."

Edith Chescoe told me, "When I was a little girl, I used to go to the Bramford's cottage with my mother. The ladies of Queenhill Women's Institute would meet there, invited by your Grandma to do sewing. They would be making things to sell—crochet items and so on. That sitting room was always used for something—Mothers' Union meetings as well.

I wasn't allowed inside, so I used to amuse myself by trying to pump water from the pump in the garden. They always had cats and chickens there, for me to look at."

Your Grandma was very good at making pastry," said Cathy Guilding. "I remember her wonderful jam tarts, freshly baked. She would come to the bottom of their long garden to bring us children some tarts."

I, her granddaughter, remember how the cottage always smelt of wood smoke, polish, and greens cooking. I loved Grandma's apple dumplings. "I like a Russet myself," said she once, peeling her Russet apple.

Grandma taught me to dance the Polka, to the music of 'See me dance the Polka' on a little gramophone record. She sang as we danced together:

"See me dance the Polka, see me cover the ground.
See my coattails flying, as I spin my partner round.
When the band starts playing, my feet begin to go,
For the rollicking, jollicking Polka is the jolliest
tune I know."

She loved the song from *Showboat,* 'Why do I love you?' and the waltz song, 'Live, Laugh and Love.' They were both on her gramophone records. Another favourite song of hers on a record was "Keep right on to the End of the Road,' sung by the Scotsman, Harry Lauder.

"Though you're tired and weary, still journey on,
Till you come to your happy abode,
Where all you love and you're dreaming of
Will be there, at the end of the road."

MY FATHER

Grandma's only son, George (my father) is here described by Austin Hartwright, who was taught by him in Upton School.

"He was a very gentle kind of man. He never got ruffled. He was never harsh with the kids, whereas the other teachers would get a bit sharp. He looked and moved around as a gentleman. We, youngsters, respected him. Like his father, he always had a smile and was gentle. I can see him now, as plain as punch."

Doreen Beach had a brother, Bill Biddle, who knew my father well, as a young man. Doreen told me, "My brother, Bill, went to Upton School, then to Hanley Castle Grammar School. He too was a pupil teacher, at Welland, before going to Saltley College, Birmingham, like George Bramford, to train as a teacher.

So Bill and your father had a lot in common. They would go to Saltley Reunions. They both loved cricket and cycled together around Upton to local cricket matches. They were both countrymen at heart."

Bill Biddle taught in three different schools in Birmingham. My father, George Bramford, taught at Cromwell Road School, Birmingham, before becoming Headmaster of Overbury School, Worcestershire, for 10 years. In 1931 he became Head of Pershore Junior School until he retired in 1951.

AUNTS

My aunts, Florence, and Winifred were very different in appearance and character. Florence was dark, destined to be a Lady's Maid, and always travelling. Winifred was fair and destined to be a homemaker, living in one place.

END OF AN ERA

1934 was a significant and traumatic year for the Bramford family. The Upton-on-Severn *Parish Magazine* for May 1934 records:

"On the 10th April when Lady Day was kept, a party of Upton's Mothers' Union members attended the Festival in Worcester Cathedral. It was a memorable occasion because our banner was carried for the first time in the Procession. The bearer was Mrs. Eva Bramford, escorted by Mrs. Bellamy and Mrs. Arthur Kent."

"The adult members of the Upton Church Choir were entertained to supper at the Rectory on April 30th by the Rector and Churchwardens. During the evening, a presentation, consisting of a silver tankard, was made to Mr. George Bramford, for his long and faithful services in the Choir."

George Bramford had sung in Upton's Church Choir for 50 years. Today, a plaque on 'his' choir stall in Upton Church records this achievement.

Grandad Bramford died on my 10th birthday, June 30th, 1934. He was aged 72. His end was peaceful but dramatic. My Grandmother had gone to the home of her brother, George Wills, in Wolverhampton, for a Reunion of the Wills family, and to meet a long-lost sister. Grandad was alone in the cottage at Upton.

Edith Chescoe remembered the occasion: "Your Granny had gone on holiday. A chappie came by the Bramford's cottage to go to the pub, and he noticed the chickens weren't outside. They were still cooped up. So he went in the pub and Dan Jakeman got a ladder up to the bedroom window and found your Grandad dead in bed."

The *Upton News* takes up the story:

"Mr. Bramford had been attended by Dr. Naish for heart trouble. A post-mortem revealed the cause of death as heart failure, and no inquest was held."

A sympathetic report of his death appeared in the Upton *Parish Magazine:*

"On the 30th June there passed peacefully away George Bramford, one of our most faithful Churchmen. He was held in the highest esteem by everyone who knew him. Modest, industrious, trustworthy in every sense, and willing to do what he could for others, he was one of those who help to make the world a better place to live in.

We shall sorely miss him from his place in the Church Choir. At the close of the funeral service, the full Choir, preceded by the Cross bearer, walked in procession to the graveside in the Cemetery, and sang the Nunc Dimittis."

The *Upton News* account revealed still further details honouring the life of George Bramford:

"He was one of the most useful and honoured men in the Upton district. He was a member of the Ancient Order of Foresters, being one of the trustees of the local Court. He had been for fourteen years Honorary Secretary of the Hook and District Pig Insurance Club. He was very fond of his garden in which he took special pride.

His services were much sought after as gate steward for local garden fetes and such like. He passed peacefully in his sleep, a very fitting end to a quiet, noble life."

My sister, Avril Bramford, recalls these childhood memories about our grandparent's cottage in Upton:

~ The Mickey Mouse toffees, which Grandma put under our pillows.

~ The small log, shaped by Grandad, for little Avril to sit on.

~ Choosing her favourite cream bun from Mrs. Round, the baker's wife's large basket of cakes and buns. This was brought to the cottage when the baker's van visited each week.

~ The farmyard smell inside the house at Portman's Farm, the home of Dan and Ruthie Jakeman, friends, and neighbours.

~ The walnut tree. It had been planted from a walnut by our father in 1900. Auntie Win said, "Major Chappell used to take home sackfuls of walnuts for his Prep. School boys in Folkstone, where I had looked after his two daughters. But the walnut tree had to come down in 1980, as it had become rotten."

~ A little brown wooden stool, hand-made by Grandad, and varnished. It was like an open box, which, when upturned, could hold dolls, as in a boat, and be pushed along on the floor.

~ The thick, embossed, green china jug, used for carrying cider for supper, from the Rose and Crown next door. The set of pink glass jugs, of different sizes, is made of Stourbridge glass.

These are my own childhood memories of the cottage:

~ "Let's go and collect the eggs in the orchard," Grandad would say. He kept his brown hens among the apple trees. But I was often fooled by the *china* eggs, placed on the straw in the coops, to encourage the hens to lay.

~ Drawing pictures on the empty pages of an old, thick, leatherbound Ledger, dating back to 1910.

~ Reading *Blackie's Annual* of 1911 with its quaintly illustrated stories and poems.

~ "Come and look at Venus!" Grandma would call out to us. And there would shine that lovely planet in the early January night sky.

~ Six-sided coloured wooden bricks, which made six large pictures when positioned correctly. These Victorian pictures showed pretty children dressed in clothes of pastel shades and riding in little carts, drawn by a St. Bernard dog, a goat, or a pony.

~ Listening to songs of the 1920s and early 1930s on old gramophone records. Our favourites were the catchy songs: 'The Wedding of the Painted Doll' and 'Who made Little Boy Blue?' I can still hear the words and music of this song:

> "In the wood, Red Riding Hood
> Said she'd tell them if she could.
> Humpty Dumpty on the wall,
> Said it was about the time that he had his fall.
> Then Little Miss Muffet confessed she knew
> And told the story to all others new,
> His love she had spurned,
> And now you've all learned
> Who made Little Boy Blue".

We also liked Jessie Matthews, happily singing 'Over my Shoulder goes one Care' and 'Dancing on the Ceiling', from her film *Evergreen.*

The wistful melody of the *Showboat* song, 'Why do I love you, why do you love me?' brings back to me the serene atmosphere of our grandparents' cottage in the 1930s.

Enid Loynes said to me recently, "As a young girl, I well remember being taken to the house where the Bramford family lived, next door to the present Drum and Monkey. Now, in 2004, when we polish the brasses in Upton Church and shine your grandfather's plaque on the Choir stalls, I do think of your family."

How inspiring and reassuring to be remembered in this way!

2 ~ My Two Aunts & Uncle

•••••••••••••••••••••••••••••••

AUNT FLORENCE—
The Aunt Who Travelled Round the World

As a schoolgirl in Upton, Florence had won prizes for sewing at the ages of 12 and 13. A Lady's Maid must be adept with her needle, to make repairs and alterations to her Lady's clothes.

It was not surprising that Florence, at the age of 16, went as Lady's Maid to Mrs. Evelyn Martin of the Martin family of Ham Court, Upton. She was with this Lady for about 25 years, until Mrs. Martin's death in Ireland.

Florence then went "on approval" to Lady Agnes Peel of Blounts, near Reading, and stayed for six years. She shuttled frequently by train, between Blounts and the Peels' large London house in Belgrave Square, constantly packing and unpacking her Lady's clothes.

When the Second World War began, Lady Delia Peel asked Florence to accompany her to Buckingham Palace, as her Lady's Maid and Dresser. Queen Elizabeth (known later as The Queen Mother), consort of King George VI, had appointed Lady Delia Peel as one of the Ladies in Waiting.

Thus began Florence's 35 years of working in the Royal Household, with numerous and varied Ladies in Waiting. She was frequently included on Royal Tours abroad, with the present Queen, the Queen Mother, and Princess Margaret.

13

Florence was ceaselessly packing and unpacking each of her Ladies' clothes, pressing them, and also looking after her Lady's jewels and coronets.

For her untiring service to Ladies in Waiting and their needs, Florence received the Royal Victorian Order from Queen Elizabeth II in 1966. This happened on board H.M. Yacht *Britannia,* in Caribbean waters, *en route* to the West Indies—a unique occasion.

Florence told me later: "The Queen said it was well deserved." One of Florence's Ladies in Waiting wrote: "Never has an honour been so richly deserved. Indeed, you ought to have the Victoria Cross for putting up with so many tiresome Ladies-in-Waiting in so many extraordinary places all over the world! And never do you seem to be unduly worried or put out. We owe you so much. I am so glad."

Edith Chescoe said, "I used to make an excuse to visit your Aunt Flo in the cottage when she returned from a Royal Tour. I wanted to hear all about it and to see all those beautiful presents given to her in those foreign countries. She was lovely!" Aunt Flo, like other staff on Royal Tours, was given commemorative medals from a variety of countries and appropriate souvenirs from Heads of State.

Lavinia Nind, who once lived in Newbridge Green, Upton, enjoyed hearing from Aunt Flo about her interesting experiences on Royal Tours. "I can tell that *you* are interested," Flo would say to her, "whereas so many people are just curious."

Lavinia continued, "Flo brought back a very pretty length of material from one of her Royal Tours. It had a pink and grey pattern, and I made a dress out of it, with a square neckline. She also gave me a very pretty fan, which was given to the ladies on board ship.

And I was presented with something unusual from a Christmas cracker from the Royal table at Sandringham. Flo said at the time, 'The contents of those crackers are far from being trinkets. They are well worth keeping!'

Once, when she and I sat talking in the Bramfords' cottage, we could smell burning. It was from Win's white cats, sitting too close to the open fire. They were scorching, and had to be moved away!"

Patrick Nance, who boarded with my aunts, recalled, "Flo would go away for six weeks and come back here for a month. She was very busy, well into her 70s, as Lady's Maid at Clarence House or Balmoral. Quite amazing really. She kept going until her very bad chill at Sandringham when she was 83 and had to retire.

Her Ladies in Waiting used to visit her here in the cottage, and also a Royal detective who lived locally. Some very interesting people came here."

Yes indeed! Aunt Flo had always been very capable and resourceful. She could cope with all kinds of situations and climates. She got on well with all kinds of people, and she had a good sense of humour.

AUNT WINIFRED—The Aunt Who Stayed at Home

Aunt Winifred, as a girl, is here recalled by Austin Hartwright, who went to school with her:

"We were the same age. I was very fond of Win. She was nice looking, with fair hair. Win was my favourite girl. While we were at school in Upton, the boys were taught separately from the girls, so we used to write notes to one another and pass them over the dividing wall of the playgrounds."

Winifred, on leaving school at 14, was apprenticed for three years to Wilcox, the milliner in Old Street, Upton. She was artistic and liked bright colours and flowers.

Edith Chescoe recalled, "When we were children, we would go into Wilcox's shop. Win would help us choose a hat for Easter Sunday. We couldn't go to church or Sunday School without a hat. They would be big straw hats with flowers round the crown."

In her early twenties, Win contracted T.B. on one lung, which was still a common illness in the 1920s. It was serious because three siblings of Win's mother had died of T.B. before they were middle-aged.

Her sister Florence told me, "Win was working then at the C&A department store in London. The surgeon, Dr. Nelson, sent her to Brompton Hospital for a year. After convalescence at Frinton-on-Sea, Win was sent home for a year and told not to work. The surgeon was pleased with her progress. She was completely cured."

Next, Win became a Nanny to the children of various families, including Jill and Elizabeth Chappell in Folkestone. Jill told me later on, "Win was a *giving* person."

When Win's father died, in 1934, she came home to look after her mother in the cottage and stayed on after her mother died. Win kept the vegetable garden going and she became a good cook.

During World War II, she cooked in a school canteen in Upton. After the war, Win worked in Ham Court Nursery, bunching flowers for market. In summer, she would have cycled to the Nursery by 4.30 a.m.

Win began to take boarders in the cottage, and they all remembered her good cooking. Jim Trevor recalled, "I stayed for several months in the cottage in the early 1950s, while I was working at Blackmore Camp. Win would ring an old school bell to get us up. She would give us a huge breakfast and hefty sandwiches for us to take for lunch.

Win would go with us on little coach outings, to darts matches in local pubs. We would return to suppers of cold meat and pickled walnuts. She would wait up for us returning from village dances at the Swan Hotel, Upton. The cinema would be open once a week.

And I remember Win's animals—bantams, corgis, white cats, and Ginger, a liver and white spaniel. And she also kept goats. She was known as 'the goat lady', and we drank goat's milk. There was an old 'watch dog' goose, Martha, out at the back. Martha lived for years.

I remember her sister Flo, who would tell us anecdotes about her royal tours, and show us photos. In January 1952, Flo returned home unexpectedly from the royal tour in Kenya, because of the death of King George VI. My friends could not believe I was staying with someone who knew the Royal Family. The Bramford sisters looked after us well. I loved the peace and quiet, and the little pub next door."

Pat Nance, another of Win's boarders, remembered, "Win liked going out and meeting people, but she also liked coming back home. She was a very good cook. That was her number 1 interest. She gave me a good evening meal.

There was the garden produce to help. The soil was good for growing peas, beans, lettuces, onions, and cabbages. But not good for carrots. There was fruit there too—raspberries, gooseberries, and an apple tree.

Win and Flo often cycled from their cottage to Malvern to

do their shopping in the 1930s and 1940s. They never owned a car."

When there was a wedding reception or a party held at the Rose and Crown, next door to the cottage, Win would decorate the tables with flowers and greenery.

Edith Chescoe, former landlady of this pub, told me, "Win made such a wonderful show, with so little to do it with. She would find all kinds of flowers from the fields, as a background to the food. And all the year round she would have flowers or flowering bulbs in her house. She used to say, 'Better enjoy them in the house than in the cemetery'."

Lavinia Nind, who knew Win well in the 1950s, said, "Win and her sister Flo were very different from each other. My husband and I were living at that time in Oak Cottage, Southend Lane, not far from the Bramfords' cottage. Win would often come to us for coffee and a chat. She was very jolly, and she loved animals.

Once, we rented a very small piece of land at the bottom of her long garden. We kept two hens in a poultry ark there. I used to pop across the road with food for them, twice a day.

I had to be very wary of Win's gander, called 'Satan'. He was well named. He would not allow anyone near his 'Bertha'. Even Win had to be very careful. Those geese were old and splendid guards. No one sneaked around *that* garden!

Now, there was the goat. Winnie had a surplus younger goat. She suggested it might be useful in clearing the ground beneath the trees in my mother's small cherry orchard in Hanley Swan.

Yes! It did just that, and every other growing thing *and* some clothes from the washing line! I'm afraid Winnie had to have it back. Incidentally, she walked the creature all the way from her cottage in Newbridge Green to Hanley Swan."

But Win's animals were useful, on occasions, as Lavinia relates. "Win helped us out once, when my cat brought all his poor mice, moles, rabbits, etc. into our house, through our bedroom window. He was aided in this by jumping first onto a water butt. We didn't mind. They were never harmed, and we simply took them back into the field behind our cottage.

But, when it came to a large *rat*, which our cat lost in our bedroom ... ! Amongst Win's pretty white cats, she had a super ratter. So in came Win, armed with a stick, and her super cat, and together with my husband, they caught and killed the wretched rat.

I can see her now. Win coming down my stairs, holding the rat by the tail, and her cat under her arm. I had stayed in the sitting room below, and from there it had sounded like the removal men were busy. Win was quite a woman!"

Winifred loved life. She was exuberant, enthusiastic, earthy, and emotional. She enjoyed the company of people and animals.

MEMORIES OF TWO GREAT-AUNTS AND A GREAT-UNCLE

Florence told me, "I had a young aunt, Rose Wills, in Bridgwater. She was my mother's youngest sister and she was a dressmaker. Once, as a child, when I visited the Wills family there, Rose made me thread needles for her and pick up pins from the floor. It was good training for me!

I also went to stay with father's sister, in Laxton, Nottinghamshire. I was there for three months, aged about 8. That was Aunt Nance. She and Uncle William were 'pillars' of the local Methodist Chapel. I had to read from a large, illustrated Bible at the family service in the house. That was each evening when we also sang hymns. One day, I went with Aunt Nance in her pony and trap to Newark Market to sell eggs and butter."

In 1981, Laxton villagers told me, "Your great-aunt Nance was a much respected, religious woman. She wore her long old-fashioned skirts, petticoats with big pockets, and her sunbonnet, right up to 1937, when she died.

She had a little shop in her house at Laxton, where she sold homemade sweets. She would give children generous portions for one penny. At Sunday School picnics, we loved her caraway seed cakes and marrow jam tarts. She used to make lovely butterscotch."

GREAT UNCLE GEORGE WILLS

"He was mother's youngest brother," said Florence. "He was only ten years older than me. He would come each summer to stay with us at Upton. He would liven up the place with his funny remarks. He was always quoting or singing from Gilbert and Sullivan operas, which he knew by heart.

He would hide a penny somewhere when he left to go home, and we children would have to find it. Once, it was poked between two pieces of wood on the yard fence. Another time, it was weeks before we found the penny—tucked under the stair carpet!"

George Wills' daughter, Patricia, told me, "As a boy, aged ten, 'Pop' had accidentally spilled red wine all down the wedding dress of his sister Eva (my Grandma). This was considered a bad omen by the wedding guests."

I myself remember this genial 'funny Uncle George', with the same twinkling brown eyes as my grandmother. He always came to stay with us in Pershore at Easter. He would often play the piano. We children would clamour for him to play "The Maiden's Prayer" and "The Robin's Return". And he would sing Edwardian Music Hall songs like "She was only a bird in a gilded cage". The Gilbert and Sullivan operas were his 'Bible'.

But he would embarrass me when singing the Easter hymns in Pershore Abbey because he *would* slur the notes together in an old-fashioned way. I can still hear him droning out "The fight is o'er, the battle done" at Evensong on Easter Day.

This Uncle, in later life, was a keen astronomer and had his own telescope in his garden. He would proclaim the wonders of Venus, Jupiter, and Mars.

He was also an avid student and reader of the novels of Anthony Trollope and Thomas Hardy. One or other of these authors accompanied him everywhere. He almost knew them by heart. But one evening, he announced with a twinkle in his dark brown eyes, and a green book in his hand, "I'm taking Mrs. Henry Wood to bed with me!"

I never knew Aunt Mabel, the third daughter of my grand-parents. She became a children's Nanny in London. But alas! typhoid fever claimed her in 1922 at the age of 27. The only memory of her that I own is a sampler, completed in about 1905 when she was aged eleven.

3 ~ The Rose and Crown Inn at Newbridge Green

• • • • • • • • • • • • • • • • • • • •

It is still there, half-timbered, ancient, at Newbridge Green, on the road from Upton to Longden, next door to Bramford Cottage, and now known as the *Drum and Monkey.*

Edith Chescoe remembered this pub in the 1920s. "We children used to go there to get stout for our parents. When we had relatives from 'Burningham' (the old pronunciation of Birmingham), and they always wanted stout. We'd go up the steps and knock on the door. Old John Fawke would come to the door and we would ask for stout.

He would bang the door shut. Then he would come back with the stout, and he always put a seal over the cork. 'Don't open the cork, he would warn us. 'Cos if a policeman sees you've opened that cork, you'll go to prison.'

What I liked about the Rose and Crown in our day was the wall around the front yard. And all the kids loved jumping that wall. Then Old John would shout at us through the window.

There were wooden benches and tables near the front steps, for people to sit, with their bottles of beer. But they drank more *cider* than anything then. Old John would please himself about when he opened the pub."

Jack Hayfield told me of his own experiences as a boy when he used to meet Old John Fawke at the Rose and Crown:

"Old Fawke was a 'nutter'," said Jack. "When I was a boy, my father had this same shoe shop we're in now. I had to deliver the shoes he'd repaired to our country customers on my bike.

I would arrive at the Rose and Crown and knock on the door. 'Who are you?' a voice within would shout. Old John, with his bushy beard, would be peeping through the curtain. 'I'm Jack Hayfield, Mr. Hayfield's son. I've brought you your shoes.'

Old John would unlock the door to let me in, and then lock it up again—quite frightening for a youngster to be cooped up with this 'nutter'! The old man would give me a small lemonade in a dirty glass, and then find the money to pay me for the repair. But on some occasions, I had to leave the shoes on the doorstep, 'cos he wouldn't open the door at all!"

Edith Chescoe continued, "The Fawke family ran that pub for quite a time. Then Old John was left there on his own. They used to make their own bread in the bakery, which is now the skittle alley. They had a little grocery shop there too. They made their own stout. We children weren't allowed anywhere near the pub—only when we had to ask for stout for our parents.

People used to say that Ada Fawke, John's sister, was a beautiful skater. Down by the Stanks was a big brook called Broadwaters. When it was iced over, she would skate there."

My aunt, Florence Bramford, had her own memories of the Fawke family, and entertainment at Newbridge Green in the 1890s and early 1900s.

"The Rose and Crown next door was kept by a family called Fawke. Anne was the mother, Ada the daughter—John and Harry the two sons. Ada and John worked in the pub. Harry was the baker because there was a bakery attached to it as well. He used to bake the bread and deliver it all around the district in his baker's cart. When we were children, our one delight was to go with him in the baker's cart to deliver the bread—for a ride in the horse and cart. We enjoyed that very much!

Old lady Fawke died in the pub, Ada died, and Harry died. Old John kept it on for quite a long time afterward. He eventually died and his nephew who had business in London didn't want it. So Dad and Win kept the pub going for about three months until it was sold.

When I was a child, Russians with a bear used to come round here. It was generally two men. The bear was chained to one man. On this corner, there was a little three-cornered piece of grass, where what we called 'the corner boys' stood while they were waiting to go into the pub.

The Russians sang a Russian drawl sort of song. This old bear would get up on its hind legs and dance with the man. The other man had a little stick and he gave the bear a little whip up now and again to make it keep on dancing.

At other times there was a man with a monkey. The man carried a funny little organ on his back and when he put it down on the ground, it stood on one stick in the middle. The organ was carried on one shoulder and the monkey was on his other shoulder. He would put the organ down and turn the handle and make the music.

You had to go up to the monkey and give it a penny. Then it would get a little paper out of the side of the organ. That was to be your fortune, you see! The monkey was dressed up in a little skirt and a sort of cape thing with a funny little hat on its head.

Then there was the German band—a brass band. It played on the corner as well. So that was our entertainment when we were children.

Haunted houses in Upton? Dick Guilding, when he was a small boy, living in Southend Farm, said to his mother, 'Who's that man who comes at the bottom of my bed?' But nobody knows who he was. It's a very old house, Southend Farm.

At Ham Court, there is the grey lady and a Cavalier soldier. My sister Win and a friend saw them going towards the river. Then there is the house in Upton called Soley's Orchard. That's haunted by its owner, Captain Bound. He was cruel and covetous. They say his ghost rides on his grey horse along the Southend Lane, where he used to remove landmarks when no one could see him."

GHOSTS IN THE PUB

Edith Chescoe and her husband, in later life, became landlords of the Rose and Crown. She told me: "On Christmas Eve when you went up the five stairs to go to bed, one stair would creak. It was Old John Fawke, we said. But you never saw him. He must have stumbled up there once. But we only heard him on Christmas Eve. The present-day landlords? Yes, I get cross with them, now I'm retired. They wrote in the paper about all these ghosties in the pub—very clever ones! There's a ghost upstairs, they say, who can take the flowers out of the pots and throw 'em about. And there's another ghost supposed to be in the skittle alley. And I get so *cross!*

I wrote to 'em and told 'em they were talking rot. I said there's only one ghost, and that's John Fawke, on Christmas Eve. 'Cos we'd been living in that pub for years and years."

WHAT'S IN A NAME?

As a child, I remember seeing Old John Fawke, in the early 1930s. He lived, elderly and alone, amid the cobwebs and dust of the unkempt and eerie tavern lit only by oil lamps.

My aunt Winifred, his neighbour, would take him meals. We children would accompany her through the back door of the pub. Old John once gave my little sister, Avril, a silver coin. A half crown was prized as a forbidden treasure in those days. So my father took charge of that coin.

Old John had the bushy grey beard of Victorian times. I remember his yellow, incredibly wrinkled old face, peering out of the shadows, and resembling that of a monkey. "He only needs a drum!" the customers would comment in their Worcestershire accents.

The newly-painted inn sign of the Rose and Crown, in pink and gold, soon sprouted a little brown drum and a little grey monkey in the bottom corners. But a few years later, when a new inn sign was commissioned, the Drum and Monkey were predominant. The Rose and Crown were demoted to the bottom corners.

"The change of name has been dictated by a piece of local folklore," remarked my aunt Florence. The 'landlord's explanation' of this change of name was somewhat different, as related by Edith Chescoe.

"During World War II, when we ran the pub, we did not get our ration of beer for the pub one thirsty week. It went by mistake to the Rose and Crown in Severn Stoke. So, Dad said, 'Why don't we call this pub by its nickname, the Drum and Monkey, to distinguish it from the other Rose and Crown?'

My Dad and nine other Upton men with a drum and monkey used to play long ago on that triangle of green at the top of Southend Lane. They were called the Drum and Monkey people. So, we got Miss Winnington, the artist across the road, to paint a new inn sign for us."

After John Fawkes's death, in about 1932, my grandfather, George Bramford, 'kept the license open' for three months. He acted as barman until a new innkeeper was appointed. They were still using oil lamps. By tradition, local farmers used to meet in the Rose and Crown to agree on the price of their hay.

THE SKITTLE ALLEY

Edith Chescoe recalled, "After Old Man Fawke died, the Simmonds took over the pub. They used the kitchen as Tea Rooms. Your aunt Win used to help them serve tea. The old bakery became the new Skittle Alley. When *we* were the landlords in the 1950s, we had parties in the Skittle Alley—all harmless fun. It would be booked for dinners by the Ledbury Hunt and local farmers. Whoever lost the skittle match had to pay for the dinners. One night, they brought in a fox and let it loose in the skittle alley!

At the back of the Skittle Alley, there were some beautiful roots of violets. You could smell their perfume several yards away. But that's all gone now."

Elsie Trapp added, "Yes, me and your aunt, Win Bramford, helped Edith here at the Ledbury Hunt dinners in the Rose and Crown. It was all men. One evening, a certain man got up and said he wanted to tell a joke, 'but there were ladies present.' So we three ladies went out of the room. But we left the door ajar.

This man saw me smiling as we came back into the room. 'You *are* naughty!' he exclaimed. 'You *heard* what I said!' 'Yes,' I replied, 'but I could have told you that one myself!'

Mr. Chescoe, the Landlord, once called me his Number Two Wife, so I was always known as 'Number Two.' It was all harmless fun—hard work, but we all pulled together."

Bramford Cottage, in the old days.

Bramford Cottage, as it stands today.

My grandparents
in the 1930s.

My grandparents at Bramford Cottage in 1895. My father, George, wears
his sailor suit and stands between Florence and his baby sister, Mabel.

Florence Bramford in
her thirties.

Florence, in her fifties,
sets off on her Royal travels.

The Queen Mother and her staff during a Royal Tour in East
Africa, circa 1948 (Florence Bramford is second from the right).

Winifred Bramford, aged ten.

Winifred Bramford with her mother at the Winter Gardens, Malvern, in the 1930s.

A Pageant held on Upton cricket ground in the 1920s
(Winifred Bramford is second from the left).

The Rose & Crown Inn (now known as the Drum & Monkey).

George Bramford, chauffeur to Lady Johnson of The Hill,
Upton-on-Severn, c. 1913

Florence Bramford posing for group photo with The Queen Mother and royal household staff at English country house.

4 ~ How Upton People Earned Their Living In Upton

•••••••••••••••••••••••

Jack Hayfield reminded me, "Upton was the last tidal port on the Severn, hence the numerous pubs. Many have now gone. The Black Boy Inn was at the bottom of New Street. The Bell was also in New Street. That is now a cafe". [The name 'Black Boy' denoted, not a Negro, but the swarthy complexioned King Charles II.]

The River Severn has been the lifeblood of Upton. Kath Hill said, "When I was a girl, in Severn Stoke, Mr. Clements was in charge of the swing bridge at Upton. He wound a handle to swing up one half of it so that barges could pass through. It took at least 20 minutes, and held up pedestrians and traffic."

Austin Hartwright confirmed this. "As boys, we used to run onto the swing bridge as it swung up—if the bridge master did not see us. The ship approaching would hoot a signal."

THE IMPORTANCE OF THE RIVER SEVERN

For the historical facts in the following three paragraphs, I am indebted to the book entitled *Upton* by Pamela Hurle.

"The Severn was a highway for commerce between many inland ports in Victorian times and in past centuries.

Corn would be carried from the Upton area downstream to mills at Tewkesbury and Gloucester. Cider from Herefordshire was transported by the Severn to other parts of the country. Goods from Wales would be sent to Upton to be carried elsewhere via the Severn. Goods arriving in Upton were taken by packhorses to villages.

In Mediaeval times, the Severn trows, twin-masted boats, would carry salt from Droitwich. Just up the river from Upton was Hanley Castle, whose potters exported their tiles and pottery, using boats on the Severn.

Long ago, the trows had to be hauled by twenty men along many stretches of river, when the wind was unfavourable. This was before towpaths were made for the later procedure of cart horses pulling barges. So these men trudged in the cold water of the river to do this exhausting work. For this, they would receive half a crown a day. They did not live long."

A local custom was to seal contracts between merchants and boatmen with a mug of ale in a local inn. A reminder of this is the Mug House Tavern in Old street, Upton-on-Severn. There is also an inn by this name on the waterfront of the once busy inland port of Bewdley.

WORCESTER ORCHARDS

Good cider, 'tis a drink divine,
Better by far than all your wine.
Good in grief, good in joy,
Good for maid, man and boy.

—*Anon.* 19th cent.

Worcestershire and Herefordshire have long been famed for their orchards of apple and pear trees. They have been equally celebrated for their cider and perry. Apple orchards existed in Saxon times and the Normans brought further stocks from Northern France.

However, the cultivation of the pear was so well known in Worcestershire that Michael Drayton in his description of the English army at Agincourt under Henry V says: "The banner of the Worcestershire men was 'A pear-tree laden with its fruit'." This very emblem remains today on Worcestershire's coat of arms.

Edwin Lees, the Worcestershire naturalist, in his *The Forest and Chace of Malvern 1877* writes: "One of the finest pear orchards in the Malvern district is by the side of the road between Powick and Newland. It is Barland Pear Orchard, with more than 70 tall trees. It is probable that these trees are more than 250 years old. The mature pear tree almost rivals the oak in majestic aspect and ruggedness of bark."

He continues, "I have observed in pastures at Mathon—old apple trees, hollow, and curiously tortuous in their holes, whose antiquity might reach beyond 300 years."

Such orchards produced a large quantity of cider and perry. Edwin Lees informs us: "A farmer residing on the borders of Herefordshire and Shropshire, the taste of whose best produce I enjoyed in the summer of 1868, told me that in a good year he made fully 300 hogsheads of liquor from his orchards, and the greater part was consumed by his labourers and his family."

Clive's Fruit Farm, on the outskirts of Upton-on-Severn, is a glorious example of flourishing orchards today.

COAL AND HAY MERCHANT

Doreen Beach told me, "My father was a coal and hay merchant. Coal was brought by boat, from Cannock to Upton. Hay was taken to Cannock in return. There were grades of coal then. Now it is rubbish—of only one kind. We had very good coal from Cannock, called 'deep screen cobbles.'

Once, in the Dudley canal tunnel, my father got his barge stuck. The tunnel was very long and very dark. He had to wait 'til the level of the canal was down, and the tunnel was passable. He and his mate had to 'leg' the barge through the tunnel, lying on the roof of the barge. My father said, 'I could have killed that lock-keeper!'"

BOATMEN AND BARGES

Kath Hill recalled, "As a child, with my 12 brothers and sisters, we lived at the Day House, between Earls Groome and Severn Stoke. It was a seventeenth-century house, where in the past boatmen used to spend the night, after bringing coal and wool in barges to the warehouses at Severn Stoke.

Donkeys were used to transport these goods between the river and the warehouses. Men would bring the donkeys up Donkey Lane laden with corn to be stored in a large barn. The corn was put on barges to be taken on the River Severn to Tewkesbury or Gloucester. Millers would grind the corn into flour.

As children, we were playing one day in the rickyards of our house. We pulled up some green weeds to be used for 'pretend cabbage,' when playing at 'houses.' Suddenly, we saw a floor of bricks beneath the weeds. When we told Mother, she said, 'That is where the stables for the donkeys used to be.'"

DOMESTIC SERVICE

"Two of my sisters became Cook and Parlour Maid at a house in Cradley, Herefordshire," said Kath Hill. "I joined them, aged 15, as a Tweenie Maid. I had to wash and iron (only flat irons then) the underwear and white silk tennis dresses of my Mistress, who played a lot of tennis. Lots of tennis parties were held at her house.

Once, using the flat iron, I scorched a silk petticoat on the front. I confessed to my Mistress, feeling *very* sorry. She replied, 'Well, it's done now. You've learned your lesson. I'm going to give you a new lace top to sew on after you've cut out the burned piece.'

I was there for two years. Then I went to four maiden ladies in Hanley Swan. But my mother was anxious, because I had a long walk there and back in the dark, up a winding lane, and across fields. So, I went next to two ladies (the Misses Salt) in Graham Road, Malvern. But I had to carry the coal and wood for fires in both lounges up from the cellar. I was not strong enough, and I pointed this out. 'We'll get someone to help you,' said my employers.

They got the gardener from next door, Reg Hill—my future husband! I used to save five shillings each week at Lloyds Bank, for six years, to pay for my wedding dress, my mother's dress, and the reception."

Advertisements for Maids in 1874:

> *Wanted in a small, quiet family:*
> a House and Parlour Maid. Steady,
> active, obliging. Neat in dress
> and an early riser.

> *Wanted: A Parlour Maid.* Must be
> a Communicant of the Church of
> England and have good references.
> Wages £16 and all found.
> [£ 16 p.a. plus board & lodging]

EMPLOYMENT FOR MEN

Kath Hill continued, "Three of my brothers worked on the land, with my father. A fourth brother became butler to a very rich Jewish family in London. He knew all about the Passover meals. His wife would make the unleavened bread. He and his wife would go on holiday with this family to the south of France!

Yet another of my brothers became chauffeur to the sister of the Duchess of Gloucester at their home in Wiltshire."

ERRAND BOY

Boys aged 12 to 15 and beyond, often worked as errand boys, delivering goods from the various shops. They were usually given a bicycle for this work, to reach customers in local villages. Jack Hayfield at the shoe shop told me, "The bike which my father bought for me to deliver the shoes he repaired—I had to pay my Dad sixpence a week towards that bike, out of the earnings he gave me—I used to cycle as far as Defford delivering shoes."

UPHOLSTERER

"My grandmother was an upholsterer of furniture," Kath Hill informed me. "She lived at Deerhurst, near Tewkesbury. And my mother left school, aged nine, to accompany my grand-mother to the big houses where she worked. This would be in about 1880.

From the age of nine, my mother would thread needles, to save time for *her* mother, who was busy sewing new covers for chairs and settees. All covers would be sewn by hand. My mother and grandmother would *stay* in these big, well-off houses for several days at a time."

THE WORK OF A PARLOURMAID

Domestic service in the homes of the gentry was the most usual work for girls who had left school at the age of 14 unless they chose to be apprenticed as dressmakers or milliners.

"My sisters went in service to the Rectory in Severn Stoke," said Kath Hill. "In fact, several of my seven sisters, as they became 15 years old, replaced each other at the Rectory.

One of my sisters was Kitchen Maid at the Lechmere's big house, Severn End. That was on the opposite side of the river from our farmhouse.

Severn End had a boathouse. On Sundays, the Severn End gardener would row my sister across the river for her time off at home. Then he would row her back again at the end of the day. He was busy gardening on the other days."

At the age of 92, Kath Hill said enthusiastically, "I've always loved housework!" She described to me her own day's work as Parlour Maid to the two Misses Salt at "Inglewood" in Graham Road, Malvern.

"I had to be up at 6 a.m. to light three fires and set the table for breakfast which was soon after 9 a.m. I had to clean the silver and glass, but another maid washed the dishes. Up until 12 noon, I wore a print dress. To wait at table for lunch, I changed to a black dress with a white apron and white headband. During the Malvern Festival of plays, throughout the entire month of August, my employers would invite home up to twelve guests to a four-course dinner provided by our Cook.

When the main course was completed, and before the dessert, I had to balance a very large tray on my palm, while collecting up all the used plates and silver. (Kath was always petite and slim). I placed this full tray on the butler's table at the side.

Then I swept the white tablecloth with a crumbs brush and little shovel and set lace mats at everyone's place ready for the fruit dessert. Each guest also had a finger bowl of water, to moisten the fingers.

Next, I had to serve coffee in the sitting room. After tidying up, I went to bed at 10 p.m. My free time was one afternoon, every other Sunday.

Every day, at 9 a.m. and 9 p.m., house prayers were held for all the household. This included the Misses Salt, the maids, the Cook, and the Butler."

Large houses, with numerous domestic staff, required the services of laundresses. Southend Lane, opposite Bramford Cottage, in Upton-on-Severn, still has a Laundry Row. The end house was the Laundry for Ham Court estate.

JOBS FOR A BOY

Austin Hartwright told me, "I went to Welland School until I was twelve. On my way to school, I went to the house of a Mrs. Moore, a widow. I did some jobs for her to earn pocket money. I pumped the water to the top of the house and got coal inside for them. On my way home, I'd get more coal and wood in for them, ready for the morning."

When Austin left school at the age of twelve, he went to work in Upton for Lady Johnson, opposite The Eades, off Monsell Lane. In 1913, he was earning about ten shillings a week, which was very good pay in those days. A farm labourer only received then fifteen or eighteen shillings per week.

Austin recalled, "I worked in Lady Johnson's house and cleaned the silver and the pewter candlesticks. I had to scrape the old wax out of each candlestick and wash them all in hot water ready for lighting candles at night.

I helped the parlour maids and cleaned the shoes. I was expected to collect letters from the Post Office from Lady Johnson's private box."

MARKET GARDENER

"In 1917, my father was a market gardener at The Hook, near Welland", continued Austin Hartwright. "The Malvern market was on every Saturday, in a big market hall at the bottom of Edith Walk. On that day, father used to ride his bicycle into Malvern, leaving me, aged 13, and my younger brother, to bring the produce to sell.

We used to pack a big old-fashioned twins' pram with our greenstuff. There was a sack of potatoes underneath on the springs and rhubarb tied on. At 7 a.m. we two boys pushed that heavy pram up into Malvern and got to the market at 9 a.m. One of us pulled it with a cord at the front, and the other pushed from behind.

When we reached Malvern, we had to take a basket each and sell the stuff round the houses in Graham Road and so on. For lunch, Dad sent us to the Gateway butcher. For three pence we got pieces of steak, liver, etc. We cooked them over a gas stove and had our meal there in the market.

Coming home at night, with the pram empty, my brother got in the pram, and I used to stand on the back, and away we'd ride down the hills to home. *That* was quite easygoing. It was fun!"

Austin Hartwright concluded, "A few years later, when we moved to Malvern, Dad became a postman. I worked with Morgan Motors in their original garage on Worcester Road, Malvern Link, tapping nuts, and putting screws on bolts. *That* was where the first Morgan car was born. Then I became a baker at George's Restaurant in Great Malvern for many years."

5 ~ Family Life and Food

Certain family names have persisted in Upton for generations—names such as Biddle, Clements, Farr, Fereday, Pumfrey, Thould, Webb ... And there were often numerous children in each family.

Kath Hill recalled, "There were thirteen children in my family—five boys and eight girls. We lived in the Day House, near Severn Stoke. It was a well-built house and was later converted into two cottages for farm workers. As our family was large, we occupied both cottages. There was a bakehouse between the cottages, which could be used by both households.

As children, we each had our own jobs to do at home—cleaning the house and helping with the animals—sheep, pigs, and geese. My mother had very sore fingers after plucking geese for the Upton Christmas market, which was off School Lane.

My job at home, as a child, was to scrub out the larder and the kitchen. On the floor stood Mother's jars of homemade blackberry and damson wine. I used to clean *around* these jars. But Mother noticed. 'That's only a cat lick,' she remarked, so I had to clean more thoroughly.

Mother's eldest son, my brother aged 19, was killed in the First World War. People would say to my mother, 'Oh, but you have other sons, Mrs. Morris.' This would make my mother furious because she valued *all* of her sons."

49

Elsie Trapp told me, "In the 1920s, wages were about thirty shillings a week. I remember a large basket of elvers (young eels) from the Severn being carried on the shoulder of a man from Gloucester. He had come by train from Gloucester, to sell them in the Upton streets. They were squirming! People flocked to buy them. It was considered a delicacy. My father used to fry them, live, in a pan."

Austin Hartwright recalled, "In the early 1900s, Mother was hard put to feed us eight children. But Lady Tennant, who lived nearby, would give us dripping from roasted meat. Mother was her dressmaker. Also, the Taylors, who had a shop, gave us good bacon dripping to spread on bread.

Breakfast would often be a hunk of bread, soaked in tea, with brown sugar on top. For mid-day, at school, Mother would give us bread and two pence each, to buy a good hunk of corned beef or cheese from a shop. Very occasionally, she would serve us a pudding made with suet. Yet we always had plenty of energy and we were happy."

Kath Hill remembered her childhood in the 1920s. "The butcher made faggots on Tuesdays—lovely and hot. We liked them! But Mother made all our bread and cakes for her thirteen children. I watched her bake and cook, and I learned how to do this from her. So I've always liked making cakes for tea.

It was a rare treat for us when we were sent once to buy a loaf from the baker's. We thought it tasted lovely—a different taste of bread for us!"

Two items of food in the 1920s were recalled by my aunt Florence when she was Lady's Maid to Mrs. Evelyn Martin. "I went with Mrs. Martin to stay with a rich lady, Mrs. Henty, in Chichester. Mrs. Henty went out each day in a carriage and pair. We visited Chichester Cathedral.

I loved their quince and apple jam. And they gave us home-made beer for lunch each day—to the butler and the maids too. That was because Mrs. Henty owned a brewery. She had a house too, in Eaton Square, London, where we also went."

Doreen Beach remembered summer food. "We did teas for hay-making. I used to take 7 or 8 bottles of tea on my bike to the haymakers on The Ham at Upton and on Fish Meadow. I can hear the *clop-clop* of the horses as they pulled the hay cart.

Our Glorster (Gloucester) relations used to come to Upton for plums in August. We collected baskets for this, made by the basket makers out of willow. The handles often wore out. Victoria plums were the best."

At Newbridge Green, my own father and his sister— George and Florence Bramford—were brought up on honey. Their father had three hives. Their mother sold honey.

Miss Anderson, from The Glebe, would make her annual visit to their cottage, before the end of May, to ask, "Have you any virgin honey?" By this, she meant early, pale honey.

In the 1890s, when my Grandad's bees swarmed, his children would run out into the garden to 'tang' the bees. Florence would bang a saucepan with its lid. George would strike a dustbin lid with a stout stick. This was to make their father's swarming bees settle in his own garden, rather than in the field or orchard. George would then run down Southend Lane, to tell a more experienced bee-keeper about the swarm. This man would arrive at the cottage to put the swarm back in the hive.

Austin Hartwright remembered his family duties on returning home from school. "In 1917, my father was a market gardener at The Hook, near Welland. He had always got a job for us boys at home, washing onions or radishes or lettuce, ready for the next day. Or we had to pick fruit—blackcurrants, plums, apples, pears. When we had picked gooseberries, we had to 'stalk and eye' them.

We sold fruit to the hotels in Malvern—The Abbey and The Foley Arms. When we boys had picked a big hamper of 80 pounds weight, we could then go out to play."

We don't hear much about Medlars nowadays, but my aunt Winifred Bramford loved them. The Medlar resembles a small, brown-skinned apple. It is only eatable when decayed to a soft pulpy state. As auntie Win used to say, "They are only ripe when they're rotten."

I have learned that one variety of Medlar is named Nottingham. This is of particular interest to me, as my grandfather, Win's father, came from Laxton, Nottinghamshire. Perhaps Win inherited her father's liking for Medlars. They may have had a Medlar tree that came from Nottinghamshire in their garden. There is a fine Medlar tree in the garden of Conderton Manor, Worcestershire.

6 ~ They Went to School

• •

Upton-on-Severn's school has always been in School Lane. In the 1890s, this Victorian building had separate areas for infants—for boys and for girls—up to the age of fourteen.

When Florence Bramford began school in 1895, at the age of four, Mrs. Priestnall, the Head Teacher in the Infants' school, had 154 infants on her books. To assist her, there was one qualified teacher and two Pupil Teachers—Julia Pockett and Rose Edwards, aged 15 and 16. They were paid the noble sum of £7 per year.

On October 24th, 1895, Her Majesty's Inspector reported: "The offices (i.e., earth closets) are extremely malodorous. They are a source of danger to the health of children and teachers alike."

The Log Book of that era includes some interesting reasons for pupils' absences. They ranged from 'Hop picking,' 'Blackberry picking,' 'Pea picking,' to 'Minding babies,' and 'Travelling on a coal barge with my mother.'

The Headmistress later recorded:

April 17th, 1896, Upton Races in the afternoon. Only a few children presented themselves. Did not open school.

A similar entry was made on the day of a Fair at Tewkesbury and a Circus at Upton.

June 18th, 1897, Queen's Diamond Jubilee. School is closed until 28th June. (Ten days!) Tea, sports, fireworks.

May 21ˢᵗ, 1900, Holiday all day to celebrate the Relief of Mafeking. Children assembled and sang 'God Save the Queen' and were then dismissed.

The role of the Rector in church schools was quite a significant one. The Rector at Upton-on-Severn took regular Scripture lessons. In the school Logbook, we read: "The Rector took the school Shoe Club money on Monday," and "The Rector sent a large basket of sweets."

Other local worthies also visited the school:

~ "Mrs. Lawson (wife of the Rector) gave the Drawing prizes."

~ "Mrs. Martin of Ham Court called and kindly promised to send plants for the school."

In classrooms, Florence and her fellow scholars were singing such songs as *The Sleigh Bells, The Scarecrow, The Minstrel Boy, I'd choose to Be a Daisy, Tit Willow, If I Were a Sunbeam.*

On Empire Day, May 24th, the girls and boys sang patriotic songs and saluted the Union Jack in the playground.

In 1902, at the age of eleven, Florence Bramford received a book for "Never missing school for one year."

Elsie Trapp's sister, Alice Hicks, was awarded a bronze medallion for Unbroken Attendance at Upton School for the year 1904-5. The medallion was embossed with the arms of the Worcestershire County Council showing the three pears.

Kath Hill told me, "I went to school at Severn Stoke. Our school stood where a large restaurant is now. There were less than one hundred pupils in the 1920s. Several came on foot from villages outside—Kinnersley, Clifton, and Earls Croome. There were no school buses then!"

Kath Hill continued, "I had the cane once! The Headmaster caned me across the shoulders for talking in class. My mother said, when she heard, that I had deserved it."

Edith Chescoe told me of her days at Upton School. "I had three brothers and four sisters. We all walked to school from Newbridge Green, where we lived. Children walked to Upton School from Queenhill and Holdfast. Mrs. Creighton was our teacher. Mrs. Harris was Head of the Girls' school and lived in the School House (now demolished). Girls went to upstairs classrooms and boys to downstairs rooms. They had separate playgrounds.

We were country children. In the winter we were allowed to stay in the classroom, by the fire, during dinner hour. Mrs. Harris used to bring us a big jug of cocoa. That was a treat! They were lovely teachers. They all looked after us.

The first lesson was Religion. But the Roman Catholics went to their morning service nearby, while we had ours.

Canon Edmundson was our vicar. He was a lovely man. When the war ended in 1918, he came into school on a Friday, and said, 'The war's finished.' We got the Union Jack put up on the flagpole and we sang the National Anthem to the flag. Then we had the day off as a holiday.

In the playground, we used to play hopscotch and tag. Tops were banned, 'cos they were afraid of the windows. We had singing games, like 'Here we go round the mulberry bush.'"

Florence Bramford recalled the 1890s. "When the floods were on, we would be watching the water every day. If the water came over the road, that meant we couldn't go to school! I always remember, once there was a big wagon that came to the school from Guildings, Southend, to take us home at half past three in the afternoon, because the flood water was coming over the road. Nobody could walk through it.

The big wagon took all the children who were coming this way through the flood water. It was very exciting for us all! Then we had to stay home for several days because we couldn't go to school. The flood used to come up quite often, but now they've cleaned out the ditches. And they've built a new road as well at the bottom of Tunnel Hill.

We took sandwiches to school every day for lunch and also an apple and a bottle of milk. Sometimes it was dripping sandwiches if Mother had nice beef dripping. Otherwise, it was a bit of bacon, but always an apple because we had plenty of those. We used to sit in the schoolroom by the fire and have our meal, then go out and play afterward."

Some pupils were troublesome:

October 18th, 1895: Punished a boy this morning for stealing sweets from a basket on the porch. This boy was punished two days ago for taking pencils from the school cupboard.

May 19th, 1896: Kate … is continually coming to school in a very dirty condition. I have had to send her home several times to be washed. Several parents have asked that their children be kept from sitting by her. I have reported this case to the Rector, the Relieving Officer, and the Nuisance Inspector.

An important and weekly feature of the timetable in the 1890s was the Object Lesson—what we would now regard as Environmental Studies. Upton's Infant School Log Book of 1893—1912 discloses an interesting list of Object Lessons that were to be taught every year:

An Umbrella	The Cow
A Postage Stamp	The Camel

The Elephant	Bees
The Ostrich	A Railway Station
The Robin	Feathers
The Baker	India Rubber
The Grocer	A Candle
The Farmer	Thimbles
The Shoemaker	The Housefly
The Blacksmith	Pins and Needles
Money	An Iron Kettle
The Clock	Moon and Stars.

The "Candle", "Iron Kettle" and "Blacksmith" jolt us right back into the Victorian era.

Miniature holidays enlivened the school routine. On Ash Wednesday, Florence and her school-mates would be shepherded to church, as was the custom for church schools. They even had a holiday for Michaelmas Day, September 29th (a Quarter Day).

7 ~ Sundays and Sunday School

• •

"Sundays were special in 1916," announced Edith Chescoe. "You had special shoes for Sunday, a special hat, coat, your knickers, your petticoat ... They were just for Sunday. And they never wore out. Children today haven't got Sunday clothes.

We weren't allowed to knit on a Sunday, or play the gramophone. Of course, the radio and television had not been invented. Grown-ups would go up in the air if you were caught knitting or playing a game on a Sunday. And we went to church three times on a Sunday. There was nothing else to do!"

Elsie Trapp joined in: "I've still got my Bible I had for good conduct, from Sunday School, and my Confirmation book, presented by Canon Edmundson. He was a lovely man. His little boy once asked, 'Daddy, why do you wear a night-shirt to go to church?'"

"The two Miss Andersons at The Glebe (on the way to Queenhill) used to take us, country children, for Sunday School," added Edith Chescoe. "That was in a cottage on the common. And if we were good, we were given a piece of cake or an orange."

My aunt, Florence Bramford, remembered *her* Sunday School in the very early 1900s. "We had to go to Ham Court, as we lived on Ham Court estate. The two Miss Bromley Martins were our teachers—Miss Madge and Miss Sue.

59

There were three classes in different rooms there—in the Smoke Room or in the School Room. We always had to learn the Collect of the day and recite it after a hymn. Then we had a reading from the Bible and another hymn.

Then we would go to the Scullery, where there was always a very large cake baked in a tin. It was a sultana cake cut into big portions. We were all given a piece of cake and a cup of milk. One day, the children threw their cake to the chickens. There were a lot of chickens there. So, the next Sunday, Mrs. Martin was there, of all people! The old lady, the mother, gave a lecture to us all. She said that if we didn't want the cake, we were not to give it to the chickens. We were not to take it at all. She was very upset. The cake wasn't baked for chickens anyway!"

It was at about this date that our famous Worcestershire composer, Edward Elgar, came regularly to Ham Court to give piano lessons to Miss Madeleine (Madge) Martin.

He would travel from Malvern by train to Upton-on-Severn. At Upton Station, a carriage from Ham Court would meet him, and take him via Southend Lane, to Ham Court and his pupil.

Children were taught to revere and respect the significant landmarks of the Christian year, and this influenced the rest of their lives.

Joan Lawrence, then in her 80s, spoke to me of the Crucifixion, with a sob in her voice. "How Jesus must have suffered!" she exclaimed.

Kath Hill, when she was aged 90, told me, "When I was in service, I was always quiet in the houses where I worked, dusting and cleaning, especially on Good Friday. I was brought up never to bang a door. Today is Good Friday. I've been thinking of the Crucifixion all day. And on Easter Day, I'll be *glad!*"

Kath had childhood memories of Good Friday. "As children, in Severn Stoke, near Upton, we would take a basket into the woods, and pick primroses for Severn Stoke church.

Mother would give us fish on Good Friday. There would be no games or jobs to do on that day—no washing of clothes or gardening.

The Festival of Easter had its own customs too. It was the tradition to wear something *new* on Easter Day. Of course, we always wore hats when we went to church.

Farrs in Upton had a nice dress shop. I used to admire the ladies' hats in a glass case in their shop window. One Easter, one of my sisters gave me a lovely hat for Easter. It was turquoise, with pink roses around the crown—*very* smart as an Easter bonnet!

And at Easter, Mother bought us a little nest of eggs from the sweet shop. She could not afford to give chocolate eggs to all of us. So, she gave us hard-boiled eggs, which she had coloured, by putting a piece of red or blue ribbon in the boiling water."

Upton's 'new' church, which replaced the old church with the 'pepper pot' tower, was consecrated in 1879. In 2004 this church celebrated its 125 years of age. Enid Loynes has listed some interesting facts about the present church building in Upton:

The Nicholson organ was transferred from the old church to the new one.

The wooden lectern, in the shape of an eagle, was carried bodily by three members of the Biddle family from the old church to the new one, to avoid it being damaged.

The chairs for the congregation, bought as a temporary measure (due to lack of funds at the time), are still being used 125 years later!

Operating the Swing Bridge c. 1920

Floods in New Street in 1924
Photographs by courtesy of John Talbot Cooper

Upton-upon-Severn Infant School in 1908.

Upton Mothers' Union with Canon and
Mrs. Edmundson and his curates in the 1920s.

Old Street, Upton-upon-Severn c.1910

Morris Dancers at the Upton Annual Folk Festival in May 2004.
Photograph by courtesy of the Malvern Gazette & Ledbury Reporter

8 ~ They Were Children Once

In the days long before our daily and familiar programmes on radio and television, films and videos, children and grownups had to entertain themselves, in a variety of ways.

"There was Morris dancing and prizes for it," said Elsie Trapp. "But it was the Waxworks that was most fun. That took place in the Memorial Hall, at Upton.

We children were all dressed in costumes from Nursery rhymes. Mr. Harris and Dr. Naish were behind us, with a comb and a matchbox. They pretended they were winding us up. My sister and I were Jack and Jill. I had to fall flat on the floor and my sister on top of me. There was Little Bo Peep too.

There were also Fetes and Pageants in the 1930s. Father Wharton organized those. He was the Roman Catholic priest. He lived in the Presbytery next to St. Joseph's Church in School Lane."

However, life in 1917 was not all play for children. There were Saturday jobs which brought in much-needed earnings.

Austin Hartwright explained: "On Saturdays when I was twelve, I used to go with a carrier, name of Bayliss—two horses and a covered-in van. We collected the skins from the butchers and packed them in the van to deliver to the tanners.

We also went to the Ice House on the Bromyard-Hereford road. There we collected two or three blocks of ice, wrapped in sacking, to bring to the butchers in Upton."

Edith Chescoe, aged 14, was sent to the big house, just across the road from her home, to be a temporary kitchen maid. "I was there for a day and a night at The Heath, where Colonel Cherry lived. And the first thing I had to do was cook a blooming partridge!

In a scullery, I had to pluck the feathers. And it smelt rotten 'cos they hang them for days and weeks. I went to bed in the servant's wing, and I cried all night 'cos I wanted to go home, and home was only across the road. But it was only for one night, 'cos the new maid come the next day."

There was quite a lot of self-made music in the Bramfords' cottage in the early 1900s, as my aunt, Florence Bramford, recalled. "Before we had a piano, our father would play the violin or the melodeon to accompany our songs and little dances. I had piano lessons until I was fourteen, and your father, George and I, as children, played duets.

As for songs, we children each had our 'party piece' solos. Mine was *Down the Vale,* George's was *Men of Harlech* or *The Lost Chord,* Mabel's was *Feed the Birdie.* And the whole family would gather round the piano on Sunday evenings, to sing hymns when we returned from church.

We would all go to The Hill on Christmas Day for our Christmas dinner, dressed in our best. That was our invitation from Sir Charles and Lady Johnson, as our father was their coachman and then their chauffeur. We each had to say a poem or sing a song for Lady Johnson, before receiving our Christmas present.

There were Christmas parties in the cottage too, as Florence vividly remembered. "The Head Gardener of Ham Court and his two children, and the blacksmith on the estate and his three children, used to come here to our cottage at Christmas.

We would have a wonderful big tea. Then it was all cleared away and we all played games. We sang to the piano and we did a bit of dancing too. It was great fun to dance with the grown-ups!

Then George and I always had to play a duet—*The Minstrel Boy*, or a lovely waltz. I played the top part and George played the bass. We sang carols too. The next day, we went down to the Watkins', the blacksmith's house, for a party. And we went on another day to the gardener's house.

Mrs. Carr, the gardener's wife, was most amusing—a very funny person. She always used to dress up. One time she came down with Mr. Carr's pyjamas on and a straw hat and banjo and she sang us a little song.

Another time, she came dressed up as a gamekeeper with a gun under her arm—anything—she used to borrow things from different people! We thought it great fun because she would disappear and we would say, 'Oh, she's gone to dress up!' And she'd come in, you see, and perform."

In summer, early 1900s, the Bramford children would be taken by train, from Upton to Great Malvern, for half a day to walk on the Malvern Hills.

"It was our greatest treat, as children," said Florence, "to go for a picnic on the hills. We would walk up from Great Malvern Station and through the Winter Gardens. There would always be a band playing on the bandstand there. Then we would climb to St. Ann's Well, where we would hire donkeys to take us up to the Beacon. The donkeys were always very docile and had keepers with them."

City children from Birmingham greatly appreciated their stay in Upton-on-Severn in the 1920s and '30s, as Doreen Beach recalled: "My brother, Bill Biddle, was a schoolmaster in

Birmingham. Once, he selected a withy stick from our garden in Upton, for a cane for the classroom.

He brought six boys from Birmingham to camp in Fish Meadow here. Part of the meadow was owned by his father. They had two tents for a week. We fed the boys—we took food out to them. We took them on walks. They had a ride to Ripple on a dray, with cart horses.

One of them wrote a good essay afterwards, about their holiday in Upton. The countryside was *new* to them. Most children from Birmingham only went away for just one day in summer, to Blackpool and the seaside—if they were lucky."

Aged eight, Florence was improving her needlework skills on samplers, at home. "Mother said I must be occupied." The sampler she embroidered at the age of nine or ten, includes two small crowns in red and the likeness of a Royal Yacht in blue—all symbols of her future. In later life, Florence was to have strong links with crowned heads and the Royal Yacht *Britannia*.

She also knitted lace. All this anticipated her apprenticeship to a milliner and her skill in repairing dresses for her Ladies.

In the days of homemade amusements, children and grownups would learn by heart the words of songs and poems, to entertain their companions on dull winter evenings. Long before the invention of radio or television, at the turn of a switch, children would recite amusing rhymes.

Here is one which my father, George Bramford recited, as a boy, whenever his mother served her family her homemade apple pie.

A Apple pie

B Bit it

C Carved it

D Dealt it

E and F Fought for it

G Got it

H Had it

I and J Joined hands for it

K Kept it

L Longed for it

M Mourned for it

N Nodded at it

O Opened it

P Peeped into it

Q Quartered it

R Ran for it

S Sang for it

T Tasted it

U, V, W, X, Y, Z
Each had a large slice
and went home to bed.

My sister and I learnt this old poem (with a moral) from our aunts.

THE CHRISTMAS CARD

Jenny bought a Christmas card and posted it to Lily.
Lily rubbed the writing out, which was rather silly.
Smoothed the place and made it neat, as well as she
was able,
Wrote 'With Lily's fondest love' and posted it to Mabel.
Mabel, who was rather mean and liked to save a penny,
Rubbed the writing out again and posted it to Jenny.
Jenny doesn't speak to Lil. Lily is offended.
Mabs, of course, is cut by both. That's how the matter
ended.

GAMES OUTSIDE

Florence Bramford told me, "We used to play all sorts of games in the garden at Newbridge Green. George and I liked to play at 'bakers' because the bakery next door fascinated us with its bread and oven. George was the 'baker' and he made mud into little loaves and put them under the plum tree to bake. I used to take them round to the other plum trees. That was the bread round!

We used to have hoops. I had a large wooden hoop and George had an iron one with a hook on the side to guide it, you see. I used to bowl my big hoop across the road and George used to bowl his so that it came through my hoop. We went all the way down the Longdon Straight with our hoops like that. So it shows there wasn't much traffic!"

A DOLL FROM CHINA

Me came floatee
In a boatee,
Muchee wavee plentee.
Voyagee over
Got to Dover,
In a trainee wentee.
Train me whirlee
Right to girlee
English girlee Missee.

Girlee shoutee
Jump aboutee
Give me muchee kissee.
Dolls she's gottee
Waxee, pottee,
Bigee dolls and smallee;
Allee samee
Me she namee
Nicest of them allee.

—Jessie Rope

That poem appeared in *Blackie's Annual* of 1911—a book carefully preserved by my grandmother for us to read. My sister Avril and I learnt and enjoyed it, as children.

At the age of 90+, my aunt, Florence Bramford, could quote no end of old rhymes and limericks, which she had collected over the years. Here is a sample:

> I went out with a duchess to tea
> I knew just how it would be.
> Her rumblings abdominal
> Were simply phenomenal
> And everyone thought it was me!

* * *

> I passed by your window and saw you undress.
> I saw you take off both your corsets and vest.
> But as I drew nearer, the fates were unkind.
> You popped on your nightie and pulled down the blind.

* * *

> There was a young man from Nepal
> Who went to a fancy dress ball.
> He went just for fun
> Dressed up as a bun,
> But was ate by a dog in the hall.

* * *

> There was an old man of Khartoum
> Who kept two black sheep in his room.
> 'They remind me', he said,
> 'Of friends who are dead',
> But he never would tell us of whom.

* * *

There was a young lady from Twickenham
Whose boots were too tight to walk quick in 'em.
She walked for a mile
And sat on a style.
She took off her boots and was sick in 'em.

* * *

There was an archdeacon who said
'May I take off my gaiters in bed?'
But the Bishop said 'No!
Wherever you go
You must wear them until you are dead'.

* * *

There was a young curate of Kidderminster
Who sadly, but surely, chid a spinster.
Because on the ice
Her remarks were not nice
When he accidentally slid ag'inst her.

Finale: Florence, whose mother was born in Devon, recited this
to her nieces on her last birthday, when she was 94 years old:

I be close on ninety-seven
Born and bred in good old Devon.
There's not a place in all the world
That can compare with Devon.
The Cornish seas be far and wide
But the Devon seas be wider
An if you'll live as old as I
Take Devon cream and cider.

9 ~ Shopping and Dress-Making

In the days before supermarkets, Upton-on-Severn, like many small towns, had several well-established little shops.

"In the 1920s, there was Eddie Webb, the tailor, on the corner," said Kath Hill. "He made suits and riding habits for the gentry. I remember he made a navy blue costume for my mother—a skirt and jacket. But she only wore it for best. As for sweets," continued Kath, "our mother usually bought a quarter of sweets per week for her thirteen children, and we had just one sweet each. But one day, a sweet shop lady gave us a large tin of Bluebird Toffees, which had been in the shop window too long. Of course, we children were delighted!

I remember the Bon Marché department store, where the Co-op is now. Biddles was the coal merchant by the river. Next to him, Mrs. Pumfrey had a boarding house. Then there was Wilcox, the draper's, and Hayfield for shoes. That shoe shop was run by the same family for four generations.

The grocer's shop was always interesting and had intriguing smells. This was because the bacon, butter, sugar, tea, coffee, rice, flour, dried fruit, etc. were all weighed out and packed up on the spot by shop assistants, according to customers' needs."

Kath Hill recalled Mr. Baker, their grocer in Upton when she was a child. "He wore a long white apron. He would ask us, children, to grind the coffee for him. We had to turn the handle of the grinder. And what a lovely smell that coffee had!"

Elsie Trapp remembered some other Upton shops. "There was Farr's for wines, spirits, and fabrics. There was a blacksmith's, Johnny Gibbs the chemist, Shepherd the butcher's, and Luther's for posh shoes. Pearce, the baker, travelled to the villages. Day's the tobacconist sold walking sticks. And the Picture House (cinema) was in the Memorial Hall, then. There were matinées on Saturdays, and for the children's matinee we paid two pence."

PUBLIC HOUSES

Being an inland port of note, Upton has always boasted a good many pubs. Several old hotels and pubs still exist—the White Lion, the Star, the Anchor, the King's Head, the Talbot, the Swan, the Plough. They are popular places on the annual occasions of Upton's Folk Festival, its Jazz Festival, and Blues Festival, as well as for visitors to the Marina.

In the 1920s, the White Lion Hotel had a tall, rounded gateway. A cobbled yard led to stables at the back. This gateway has now been filled in and the Pepperpot Bookshop stands in its place. Kath Hill related, "Me and my older sister had to go to the White Lion, to pay our father's Club money. It was a Provident Club, in case of illness. We children had to go up this yard to a room at the back. But we didn't like doing this, 'cos there was all men in that room. However, the man taking the money would call us children forward to his desk, ahead of all the other men. So it was all right then."

Kath Hill added, "My father, although he was a farm worker, was a Conservative all his life. He paid into this Provident Society, run by the Conservative Club of Upton. He used to explain: 'I'm a Conservative because I prefer to have someone above me who is educated and knows what he is doing'."

DRESSMAKING

One hundred years ago, it was quite usual to buy material for clothes and employ a dress shop or a private dress-maker to take your measurements and make up your clothes. This practice continued up to and during the Second World War and beyond that.

My aunt Florence, at the age of fourteen, in 1906, was apprenticed to an Upton dress-maker and milliner, named Mrs. Hartwright. This lady lived on the other side of Upton's old stone bridge. Florence would have to walk there and back every day from her home in Newbridge Green.

"Dad used to escort me home in the evenings," Florence told me. "He used to meet me in the town at half past six because there were no streetlamps at all! Once you left Upton Bridge, you were in darkness. So, Dad walked home with me."

Florence was later to use her sewing skills in repairing and altering the dresses of Ladies in Waiting to the Queen.

Doreen Beach told me about some Upton dressmakers in the 1920s. "Miss Bradley made clothes for the Coventrys and the Hutchinsons (the Upton Vicar and his wife). She was known as 'The Court Dress-maker.' She made baby clothes too. For me, she made frocks. And in 1938 she made my last suit—a skirt and jacket.

Farrs, at their shop in Upton, sold crepe de chine at five shillings and eleven pence per yard. You would need 2½ yards for a dress. They would charge seven shillings and sixpence to make up a frock. Tucks and pleats would cost half a guinea extra. On the invoice, they added one and a half pence for half a reel of thread and, of course, the buttons would be extra.

Palmers in Worcester sold green crepe de chine. Once, I bought enough for a blouse top and a matching pleated skirt. It cost twelve shillings and sixpence for Miss Bradley to make it up. It was ever so pretty. It was my best frock for my holiday."

Austin Hartwright, the son of Florence's dress-maker tutor at Upton told me, "We lived in Malvern during the First World War. My mother would send me, as a schoolboy, to a house in Avenue Road, Malvern, with a large box of finished dressmaking. My mother would say to me, 'Wait for the box!' (meaning the payment too)."

But Austin would often have to return home *without* the payment, on which his mother relied so much to feed her eight children. He would see his mother's face grow sad when he returned home.

Large families had to make do with 'hand-me-downs.' "Our clothes were handed down from sister to sister," Kath Hill told me. "And I had seven sisters. Mother would make a child's nightdress from a grown-up's old one. She knitted pullovers and socks for all thirteen of her children.

One of my brothers was butler to a rich Jewish family in London. They would send us lots of lovely second-hand clothes, and expensive cast-off shoes—even discarded school uniforms. We were indeed grateful.

I *did* feel smart in my second-hand gym slip, 'cos there was no school uniform in Severn Stoke School then. Those London clothes were made of very good quality wool, cashmere, and silk. We were sent lovely tweed skirts and cashmere sweaters.

Mother was very good at adapting second-hand clothes. She was once given a man's suit—a cast-off from the gentry.

She carefully unpicked it and made from it a suit to fit one of her sons for his confirmation.

And, of course, you always had to wear something new for Easter—even if it was just a cast-off hat, freshly trimmed. As for shoes and boots—there were Shoe Clubs where you paid in a weekly sum, to save for a much-needed pair of shoes."

Let Elsie Trapp have the last word on clothes: "When we girls left school, in Upton, at the age of 14, we were given a big bundle of material from Farr's shop. It was enough to make a dress. It was a present from the school.

There were lots of dressmakers in those days. And my sister was getting married. I was given enough material to make me a two-piece to go to her wedding. Fortunately, my oldest sister was a dressmaker."

10 ~ Journeys

• • • • • • • • • • • • •

Travelling on foot was the commonest, cheapest, and most acceptable way in the early 1900s. Most people could not afford a bicycle. Cars had only just been invented. Only the gentry could afford to own a motor car.

"We used to walk from Upton to the little village of Bransford to see our grandmother," said Edith Chescoe. "Bransford lies between Malvern and Worcester. That would be about 12 miles from Upton."

Elsie Trapp told me, "My mother came from Pershore. As a girl, she used to live in Priest Lane there, and her mother still lived in Upton. So Mum would walk from Upton to Pershore (about 12 miles) pushing a pram! Sometimes, a market cart and horse, taking produce to Pershore Market, would give her a lift."

Jack Hayfield said, "My father and his friends from Upton, in the 1920s, would walk to pubs as far away as Longdon or Severn Stoke. There was a Club at Severn Stoke, called the Good Shepherd. Every week, the Club gave to each of its 20 members, in turn, a new pair of shoes. They would need them because Upton workmen walked long distances to their work.

I recall in the 1920s, workmen walking from Upton to Stoke Edith in Herefordshire, to work at Lady Foley's house and estate. They would stay there all the week and walk home again at the weekend."

In 1916, when he was about twelve, Austin Hartwright used to travel and work with carrier Bayliss of Welland, on Saturdays. He had two horses and a covered van.

"On Saturdays, we took old ladies shopping in Worcester. Arrived in Worcester, we would put the van and the horses in the stables of the Swan with Two Nicks pub in New Street. That carrier's cart was like their local bus—their only way of getting to Worcester from the villages. And Worcester was a better shopping centre than Tewkesbury. Then we delivered the old ladies back to their village homes in the evening."

Austin Hartwright remembered hard winters in about 1917. "We were living near Welland. Father always sold his vegetables and fruit in Malvern—never in Upton or elsewhere. We set out with the horse and cart in all weathers. We would start off in the snow from Upton. All the way up to Malvern you had to stop and clean out the hooves of the horses.

The snow ploughs with three horses had been up in West Malvern early at 6 a.m. And down the Wyche, the snow used to be 5 or 6 feet high on either side of the road."

People who could afford to buy a bicycle in the early 1900s made the most of their opportunities for travel. They thought nothing of cycling from Upton to Birmingham and back, on fairly quiet roads, troubled only by horses and carts, and an occasional motor car.

My aunt, Florence Bramford, recalled staying with her lady, Mrs. Evelyn Martin, for three months in Homme House, Much Marcle, Herefordshire. Several of the staff were from Upton, including Lydia Webb.

"We would all cycle home to Upton from Much Marcle on a Sunday once a month," said Florence. "We would set off at 10 a.m. to cycle the 17 miles home. It would take us 2½ hours.

Then at around 6 p.m., we would all cycle back together, via Ledbury."

At the age of 18, Florence accompanied Mrs. Martin to live for five years (1906-1911) at Sarn Hill House, Bushley. They rented this house from the Dowdeswells.

"We used to cycle from there in all weathers to dances at Forthampton Court," said Florence. "There would be the domestic staff of Forthampton Court there and the gardeners and so on. Lady Yorke of the Court would be present too. She was a Lady in Waiting to Queen Mary.

When we had laid out our ladies' dresses for the evening, we Upton people would cycle home every Sunday afternoon. There would be Lyd Webb and two other lady's maids and me. We would cycle to Upton via Pull Court and Queenhill."

My aunt Winifred told me, "Flo and I would often cycle from Newbridge Green to Malvern, to shop, in the 1930s and '40s. And with the Smith family from Southend Lane, we would all cycle to White Leaved Oak, under the Malvern Hills, by way of Longdon Marsh. We would have a picnic in the bluebell woods."

Doll Smith recalled, "In the 1930s when we were school-children, we all had bikes. My family would cycle to Weston-super-Mare from Upton for our holidays. We did that four years running. The roads were quiet then. We would set out early and take lots of sandwiches with us. We would go so far and rest, and we always used to stop at Clifton, on Bristol Downs.

We went the Maisemore Way, to Corse Lawn, and through to Gloucester. Then we took the old road to Weston that is now a by-pass. We would stop in a village and walk round, reaching Weston by tea-time.

Mother used to take my two brothers and me to Weston for four weeks of Bed and Breakfast. The reason was that my father was a Scout Master. He would take his Scouts to Lydney first and join us for the second two weeks in Weston."

My own father, George Bramford, never owned a car. We were brought up to walk or cycle. In the 1930s and '40s, we used to cycle from Pershore where we lived to Newbridge Green, Upton, to visit my grandma. Our usual stop, *en route*, was at the Jockey Inn, Baughton. My father would go inside to the bar, for a beer or cider. My sister, Avril, and I would sit outside to drink our lemonade.

The age of the motor car dawned in Upton in about 1912. Dr. Naish, the local doctor, was one of the first to own a car, and drive to see his patients. His car had an open top and a canvas hood. It was now time for coachmen to be transformed into chauffeurs—almost overnight.

In about 1912, Florence's father, George Bramford, like many other coachmen, was sent to the Austin works in Birmingham, to stay for a week or two. He had to learn not only how to drive, but also to maintain Colonel Johnson's newly-acquired motor car.

Then a Birmingham man came to stay at The Hill, in Upton, for a month, to instruct and accompany the newly fledged chauffeur, Mr. Bramford, as he drove his master in the new vehicle, at 30-40 m.p.h. through the Worcestershire lanes.

Florence Bramford, too, learned to drive a car in the 1920s—in Ireland. It was Mrs. Evelyn Martin's Rover with a hood that rolled back. During her six weeks holiday back in England in 1928 with Mrs. Martin, she was taken to Cheltenham to hire a car from Haynes and Strange, so that she could get further driving experience.

Florence remembered with what pride she drove her parents from their Newbridge Green cottage through Tewkesbury to Overbury at the foot of Bredon Hill. They were visiting her brother, George, his wife, and little their daughter aged four, in the School House at Overbury.

As a small child, I can dimly remember this auspicious occasion. I had scarcely seen a motor car close up before. The cars owned by the Holland Martins of Overbury Court went slowly and smoothly past our house. But this one was actually parked in our school playground!

Of course, no driving test was needed in those pre-war days. You just bought a license for five shillings and a friend or relative gave you driving lessons.

And buses? One day, in the early 1930s, when I was eight or nine, Grandma Bramford took me on the bus from Newbridge Green to Tewkesbury. This was a new route for me. It was a popular bus service. The bus went via Longdon and Bushley and was *full* of passengers. We shopped in Peacocks Department store when we reached Tewkesbury.

And trains? I remember being taken by train in about 1935 by aunt Win from Upton-on-Severn to Great Malvern. This was in the school holidays and in those days that section of railway still existed.

We went to Malvern cinema, especially to see the black and white film *Midshipman Easy*. Afterward, we visited Woolworths and the Dorothy Café in Church Street, run by Miss Schneider and renowned for its delicious Viennese cakes. All this was a *great* treat for me because we did not often go to the cinema and there was no Woolworths in Pershore where we lived and no Dorothy Café.

But let us return to the old days, recalled by my aunt, Florence Bramford. "I would see Father, sometimes, riding one horse and leading another as he exercised them down Southend Lane, opposite our cottage, or took them to the blacksmith at Longdon Heath. He would return home at the end of the day, smelling of horses and polished leather and still wearing his leather gaiters and strong boots.

Best of all, George and I were allowed to ride in a cart with Dad on special occasions. I remember how we would meet a train at Christmas and collect parcels of food for the Home of the Good Shepherd at Welland. My father's Lady Johnson was Patron of this Home. We children, wrapped in traveling rugs, would accompany Dad in the open cart along Hanley Road and back through Welland."

As a baby, Florence made an unusual journey—a mode of travel that she was never to repeat. One winter's day, she was wheeled in her wooden pram by her mother, right onto the River Severn at Upton, and across to the other side. The river was frozen over! Her father and others skated seven miles down the River Severn to Tewkesbury in the great frost of 1891.

11 ~ How They Coped with Illness

• • • • • • • • • • •

Home remedies were highly prized in the centuries before the National Health Service came into being.

My grandmother's remedy for a bad chest cold was home-made Raspberry Vinegar and Blackcurrant Tea. If you had a sore throat, my aunt Winifred advised the old remedy of wrapping round your neck a stocking you had worn that day when you went to bed.

Before the discovery of antibiotics, my aunt Mabel had died of Typhoid fever in London in 1922, at the age of 27. She was a children's Nanny. "It was because the drains and sewerage were so outdated in those days," said my grandmother.

They told me that at the age of thirteen, Mabel had been awarded at school, a prize for Buttonholes. She had also received a book prize for one year's unbroken attendance at school. There was a photo of her on the wall, looking serious and rather apprehensive. Otherwise, the family did not talk about her.

Long ago, parents dreaded epidemics as well as the doctor's bill. A visit to the doctor cost two shillings and sixpence in the early 1920s when a farm labourer only received 18 shillings a week.

Sick people often bypassed the doctor then, and went to the

local pharmacist for medicines. If they were too poor to pay in money, they would bring the pharmacist eggs from the farms, or pheasants poached from the woods.

On October 15th, 1894, Mrs. Priestnall, Headmistress of the Upton Infants' School, wrote nervously in the School Log Book. "Because of Scarlet Fever, the classroom has been well disinfected with carbolic acid and a wet sheet hung there."

Elsie Trapp told me, "When I was ten or eleven, I was in Upton Isolation Hospital for eight weeks with Scarlet Fever. My brother was there for ten weeks. There was a separate ward for Diphtheria too. They had a special horse-drawn cab to fetch us from home to the hospital, to avoid infection. All the beds were full.

I remember one of the nurses cleaned the floor of our ward with a great big bumper thing on a stick. She used to get one of us kiddies to sit on it to polish the floor!

Our house had to be disinfected. My sister, aged 8, at home, was having a bad time—worse than we were. The disinfectant had got into her system and caused her to have great blisters all over. It must have been a very strong carbolic. Long after we came out of the hospital, she had to go to Worcester Infirmary for treatment. She had to have a pillow between her legs in case she burst the blisters.

Edith Chescoe added, "My Mum used to be one of the washing ladies at that Isolation Hospital. She used to walk from our house, along Wheatley Lane. She did the washing there for three days a week, and she was a whole day doing ironing. They were hard days, but we all enjoyed ourselves."

Upton's Isolation Hospital was on Welland Road. Its location is now called West Bank, where houses are built on the site.

Those were the days when most babies were born at home, attended by the local midwife. She would arrive in a pony and trap, or on a bicycle.

Here are some old remedies of the early 1900s recalled by Uptonians:

To cure a cold on the chest:
Rub chest each night with goose grease.

To relieve Bronchitis—make a Poultice:
Take a piping hot cloth steeped in bread and mustard, or, in flour and linseed, and apply it to the chest and back for several minutes.

To cure Chilblains on the foot:
Rub a raw onion on the chilblain.
Or put your foot in a full chamber pot.

12 ~ The Gentry

• • • • • • • • • • • • • • • • • •

"Your family, Margaret, have such a reverential attitude towards the gentry," said Doll Smith to me one day. And no wonder! My Bramford grandfather, grandmother, and aunts had all been employed for a lifetime in the service of people who lived in big houses and could afford to keep numerous domestic servants.

By association, some of the gentility of these well-endowed ladies and gentlemen rubbed off on the Bramfords of Upton-on-Severn, whom neighbours respected for their reliability and kindness. They acquired a simple dignity and showed the same consideration to others as had been shown to them by their genteel masters and mistresses. Likewise, their colleagues, who were also 'in service' all their lives, displayed the same disciplined character.

At the early age of six, Florence Bramford was to have her first taste of service to the Martin Family of Ham Court. The Martins owned the Bramfords' cottage, among very many on the Ham Court estate.

A grand wedding took place in Upton-on-Severn on November 4th, 1897, when Miss Eleanor Mary Bromley Martin of Ham Court married Mr. Robert Holland-Martin of Overbury Court, Worcestershire in the new parish church of Upton.

Little girls aged five or six, living on the Ham Court estate, were selected (or perhaps requested!) to be flower girls at the wedding. Florence was one of these.

She remembered it vividly. "We were all dressed in white. There were about six of us. We had white baskets and white flowers and we had to strew the flowers in the aisle when the bride came down after the wedding. Outside the porch, there was an awning down to the gate.

From the porch, under the awning, stood a file of older girls, up to twelve or fourteen years of age. They were dressed in red cloaks with green hoods. That was the livery colour of Ham Court. They had chrysanthemums of that shade—red, brown, and bronze, which they strewed where the bride walked under the awning down to the gate. It was in November and it was a lovely day." A very Victorian wedding indeed!

Six sons were subsequently born to Mr. and Mrs. Robert Holland-Martin: Geoffrey, Edward (known as 'Ruby'), Cyril, Deric, Thurstan, and Christopher. Florence Bramford was destined to make frequent stays at Overbury Court, their family home, in the course of her duties, later on in her life.

Austin Hartwright was proud and pleased to work for Lady Johnson of The Hill in Upton when he was thirteen and had left school. He earned ten shillings a week.

"I helped the parlour maids and cleaned the shoes," he told me. "I was expected to collect letters from the Post Office, from Lady Johnson's private box.

She was a smart lady, Lady Johnson, a nice old soul, very active. It was 'Yes, my Lady; no, my Lady, of course. Then I would help the gardener, Ernest Bennett, to sift soil and pot geraniums. Another job was to feed the geese.

I well remember the Daimler, because I had to help your grandad, George Bramford, the chauffeur, to clean it. But I never had a ride in it. Your Grandad was always polishing it, ready for Her Ladyship's drive out. He would drive her to Upton, Hanley, Ryall, or Malvern. She was always going out for a drive.

Lady Johnson would visit friends in other big houses—the Grice Hutchinsons at The Boynes (and they had a butler who was a foreigner), the Isaacs at Boughton, the Cherrys at Renwick; or to catch a train at Upton Station."

Kath Hill recalled, "The Coventrys owned all the land around us at Severn Stoke. When I attended Severn Stoke School, two of my fellow pupils, a boy and a girl, were the children of the butler at Croome Court, the seat of the Coventrys.

Every day, this boy would bring me a carnation, and I would take it home. The carnation was the daily buttonhole of the Earl of Coventry, which he had discarded the day before.

Canon Coventry (a relative of the Earl) was a priest at our church at Severn Stoke. My mother had asked him to be my godfather. His present to me, as a small child, was a little pink cup and saucer. I still have it in my china cabinet. Every Sunday, as a child, I would drink tea from it."

Joan Preece of Malvern told me, "All my Dad's brothers were tailors. My uncle, Willy Walton, kept this little shop in Old Street, Upton-on-Severn. He done quite a lot of work for the Coventry family. In those days, their riding habits were handmade. He had to go to Croome Court to measure his clients. He was a very busy man, Uncle Willy.

In Hartlebury Castle Museum, I found this sign: *Walton, Breeches Maker*. That was Uncle Willy. And there was also a fox's head in that Museum, that he used to have in his shop window, and a hunting cap."

Edith Chescoe remembered, "Ham Court had an icehouse in the wood there. It was where they kept the ice blocks to preserve the food—like in a fridge."

Austin Hartwright too had a link with Ham Court: "My grandfather was the estate carpenter. He made all their own gates and doors. At the Stanks, I recall seeing the Ham Court dog kennels. That was for their hounds, for hunting."

At King's End, Powick, in the 1920s, lived several well-off people, who employed maids and butlers, and chauffeurs. Sir John and Lady Sumner, the Typhoo Tea people, lived at Ham Hill, King's End. In 1928, Kath Hill, aged 16, was their housemaid. While there, she was confirmed at St. John's Church, Worcester.

Kath told me, "Lady Sumner attended Powick Church, but never Sir John. Nevertheless, he was generous in giving money to Powick Church. *His* Sunday morning was spent snipping and tidying the yew and box trees in his garden. They were his topiary, in the shape of peacocks, etc.

On my Sunday on duty at Ham Hill, Lady Sumner would say to me, 'Would you like to go to Evensong, Kath? You can lay the table for supper when you get back. And you can sit in our pew in Church.'

Samples of their Typhoo Tea would come from their tea plantations in India, packed in little canisters inside linen bags. These would arrive in a special post bag, locked. Sir John had the key. Lady Sumner would give me a packet of tea to take home to my mother in Severn Stoke. That was good!"

From the gentry whom they served, the humbly-born learned much. They heard and saw people more educated than themselves. They unconsciously imitated their speech and manners. Visitors to the house from elsewhere in the country, or from overseas with their retainers, would broaden the horizons of Worcestershire people in service.

If your employer was kind, it was an interesting life, especially if you were a Lady's Maid. You would accompany your Lady to stay at other large houses owned by her friends or relatives.

More experienced Lady's Maids would teach a fledgling Lady's Maid how to fold and pack her Lady's clothes, and on arrival, how to press them, ready for wear. Ladies' Maids had to look after their Lady's jewelry too.

A housemaid or Lady's Maid would, by long association, assume unconsciously her Lady's gracious ways, and between herself and her genteel Lady, there would exist a mutual esteem.

It was a sociable life and a status symbol to be serving the gentry, alongside staff whom all took a pride in their work. If you had a kind and reasonable employer, you benefited from good accommodation, ample meals, companionship, and travelling to unusual places. Such a plethora of servants was once employed in the big houses, that life was never dull. As a life-long Lady's Maid, Florence Bramford remarked, with a twinkle in her eye, "It was all great fun!"

Kath Hill's large family of thirteen children (see photo) all worked for the gentry, from the age of fourteen. They became butlers, parlour maids, or cooks. Kath's mother was a good cook, so her eight daughters all learned how to cook from their mother.

May, the eldest girl, became a Housekeeper. Chris was chauffeur and groom to Lady Sybil Phipps of Westbury, Wiltshire, sister of the then Duchess of Gloucester.

We will let Kath Hill have the last word. "At home, we each had to lay the table in the correct way. If it was not right, Mother made us do it again. She trained us all well. Many people used to say to me, 'Kath, you must have had a wonderful mother!'"

13 ~ Anecdotes: Amusing and Serious

· ·

Kath Hill shared these four memories:

DOWN A RABBIT HOLE

"We children were running through the fields. I was wearing a pair of new shoes. Suddenly, one of my shoes came off. It had caught in and fallen down a rabbit hole!

My brother ran back home and brought some fire tongs for us to pull it out. But the tunnel was too deep. My nice little shoe was gone forever!"

FIRE!

"One early summer morning, at our house in Severn Stoke, my mother saw a great light through the open bedroom window. Our hayricks were on fire!

My brother ran into Upton to the fire station to break the glass on the door and sound the alarm. The horse-drawn fire engine was slow to come. They used hand pumps in those days. Not much hay was saved.

We think the fire was lit in revenge by a tramp. He had called at our door. My mother would only give food and drink to tramps—never money. And she told us that this tramp had been furious when she had refused him money."

ONE FOGGY NIGHT

"One winter's night, when I was in my 40s, I walked from Holly Green, on the other side of Upton-on-Severn, back home to Malvern Link. That would be about 10 miles. It was a foggy night and I had presumably missed the last bus home. I refused a lift offered me near the Rhydd. When I reached Barnards Green, I caught a bus to Malvern Link.

Some children on the bus were staring at me and laughing. I heard them say, 'She looks as though she has slept for a hundred years!' And in the bus window's reflection, I caught sight of myself shrouded in a foggy mist, covered in white wisps of fog. The next day, the bus driver apologized for my long foggy walk. He said his bus had not been able to set out at all—because of the thick fog!"

THE SEVERN IN FLOOD

"At Severn Stoke, the river often burst its banks and flooded the fields. But it would never come right up to our house.

Once, my father and brothers had to rescue our horses, who were terrified of the flood. Our geese actually swam across the swollen river to Hanley Castle. But my mother called them back and they did return."

KEEP YOUR HAIR ON!

Austin Hartwright recalled these two experiences:

"In the early 1900s, we Upton schoolchildren were taken to a field to play football. Fred James, our teacher, used to wear a wig. One day, the football hit his wig and knocked it off. He was trying to put it back on without us seeing. He thought we did not know he wore one. But we *did*. It was quite funny!"

A TOUCH OF MAGIC

"I had a wart on my thumb. People advised me to go to a Wart Charmer. He lived at the Lodge leading to Ham Court. So I went to see him.

Inside his cottage, I saw him sitting in his armchair. 'Come 'ere!' he said. He muttered something over my thumb. He had warned me in advance, not to say thank you to him: So, I didn't thank him. Do you know, he charmed my wart away!"

ANCIENT WEAPON

Pat Nance told me, "In your Grandad's cottage in the back workshop, I was surprised to find a Boer War bayonet. It was up in the eaves and was quite long. Some old soldier had left it there, perhaps."

DOCTOR NO

Doreen Beach recalled a childhood memory. "Our home was Bridge House, very near to Upton's bridge. Dad's horses for his barge were stabled round the back of Bridge House.

Across the road from our house was the home of Dr. Naish, Upton's medical doctor. I was the only girl among four brothers and two cousins. I used to go with them to cricket matches and I was always the one who had to fetch the ball if it got lost.

One day our ball was thrown into Dr. Naish's garden. I crawled under the hedge to get it. But I got caught!

Dr. Naish was a big, towering man. 'You don't mind, do you?' said I nervously to him. 'Yes, I *do,*' he replied. 'Next time that happens, your brother should come and fetch it himself.' We were very careful after that."

THE RED AND THE WHITE

Cathy Guilding told me, "I was confirmed during World War II, and my confirmation dress was made out of white parachute nylon. Lots of people acquired one-eighth of a parachute in those days of clothes rationing to make a dress or blouse.

Your aunt Flo, a skilled dressmaker, was making the dress for me. When I called at your Grandma's cottage to try the dress on, Flo happened to prick her finger and the blood ran all down the white nylon! We eventually got the stain out—but I shall always remember that."

A GLIMPSE OF THE PAST

My sister, Avril, tells of this experience. "One bright sunny day in summer, I was walking from Upton to Newbridge Green along Southend Lane. There was no one about, but before I reached Southend Farm, I had a feeling of crowds of people in the fields on either side of me.

I think it was a vision of Royalist soldiers, camped in those fields at the time of the Civil War in Upton. After all, there was a battle on Upton bridge."

My aunt, Florence Bramford, related these three anecdotes:

LOST AND FOUND!

"Mrs. Johnson, wife of the Station Master at Upton Station, had been picking plums and packing them into hampers to send by night train to Manchester.

Her wedding ring had come off during the process and it had fallen, presumably among the plums. She phoned the station in Manchester, to tell them. After the plums had arrived in Manchester and had been emptied out, the Manchester people burned the hampers, and there was her wedding ring, among the ashes!

Dan Jakeman of Portman's Farm, Newbridge Green, found a missing gold cuff-link in debris dumped on his land. It had been lost in a fire at the nearby thatched cottage.

One of my Ladies lost a ring. Soon afterwards she gave me an old handbag to throw away. I thought it wise to search every part of the handbag first—and I found the missing ring!"

Florence Bramford had a wealth of little stories to relate about her interesting life as a Lady's Maid to a variety of Ladies. Here are some of them:

WHITE GLOVES

"Mrs. Evelyn Martin, whom I looked after for 25 years, was very fastidious. She used to wear a clean pair of white gloves, every time she went to the lavatory. And I had to wash and dry each pair!"

THE FRENCH WAY OF LIFE

Lady Agnes Peel took Florence with her to Cannes in the south of France in the 1930s to stay in a villa. The French cook and her husband, who doubled as butler-cum-chauffeur, were always quarrelling about 'Mademoiselle Bicyclette.' She was a French girl who came every day on her bicycle to clean the villa. Plainly, the cook was jealous of 'Mademoiselle Bicyclette.'

Florence had to go to the Cannes market to buy three chamber pots for use in the bedrooms. She had to carry these three items home, 'naked' and unwrapped, because there was, of course, no wrapping paper in the marché!

When they visited Grasse, 'la ville des parfums,' Lady Agnes Peel asked Florence, 'Where does this place remind you of?' Florence looked at the hills and said immediately, 'Malvern in Worcestershire—back home!'

14 ~ Round the World with the Royals

• • • • • • • • • • • • • • •

Here are some anecdotes about Royal Tours 1947–1982, related by Florence Bramford. She was, on numerous occasions, Lady's Maid to Ladies in Waiting to Queen Elizabeth II, or the Queen Mother, or Princess Margaret.

THE ROYAL TRAIN

On Sandringham Station, Queen Elizabeth II was holding little Prince Edward in her arms and she had young Prince Andrew by her side. The Queen was saying to Prince Andrew, 'Come and see this lovely steam engine. We shall soon have no more of these.' But Prince Andrew was more interested in looking at Florence and others of the Royal Household, who were already on the train!

HOLIDAYS IN BALMORAL

"At Balmoral the red squirrels were tame," said Florence. "They would come on the flat roof and we would feed them on rock cakes specially made for them by the cook."

Even in her nineties, Florence still received postcards from her Ladies staying in Balmoral. 'I do wish you were there at the end of the corridor.' 'Lots of fishing and picnics here every day.'

LOOKING AFTER LADIES' DRESSES

Florence told me, "One crisis involved a dress stained with motor oil, in Panama. Owing to the exuberant crowds breaking ranks, one of the Ladies had been forced to move among the motorcycle escort and had a black greasy mark on the hem. I remembered that 'Tide' had been used once, on board ship, to eradicate a tar stain. So I used this 'neat' successfully on the oily mark.

We were in Rome once, on a State Visit, when a zip stuck in the dress being worn by Lady Abel Smith. The Italian House-keeper of the hotel came up and said, 'I'll get your dress taken to one of the dress-making houses in the city for a new zip.' So, she had it in a box and it was brought back as good as new next morning.

In Ceylon, we went up into the hills for the weekend, on a special train, laid on by a Ceylon tea plantation owner. So we had a lovely rest up there, all of us, out of the heat.

Then a notice came round to our rooms to say, 'Any dresses to be washed, or gloves to be cleaned, should be put out in the morning and they will be returned in the evening.' I was with Lady Pamela Mountbatten, so I put out six dresses of hers, four of my own, and some gloves of hers. They were all washed and brought back that night. Marvelous really!

During a tour in The Gambia, we all went in barges up the river, where the crocodiles are hunted. It was an all-day trip of seventeen miles. The Queen's barge went ahead, but ours was delayed at one point by a fallen tree. We were too high to go under it. We only returned to the *Gothic* at 8 p.m.—too late to dress our Ladies for dinner.

So, the valets of the party, who were already back on board

the *Gothic*, joked that they had been combing Lady —'s hair and they had been running Lady—'s bath instead of us!"

DIAMOND TIARAS

Once, Florence had to take her Lady's diamond tiara to bed with her, for safety, as there was no access to a safe until morning. Another time, Florence was carrying a diamond tiara off the Royal plane. Her Lady had just taken it off. A steward came forward and asked her if he could look more closely at it. 'Are they real?' he asked. 'That's my nearest look at real diamonds!' he exclaimed.

KENYA

"The pilot of the Royal plane flew us right round Mount Kilimanjaro for a close look inside the volcanic crater. It was filled with snow!"

CANADA

"From Prince Edward Island, we had sailed in *Britannia* right up the St. Lawrence River to Ottawa. I always remember the maples turning colour. It was absolutely gorgeous—the different shades, from flame to deep gold.

Once, we were in Edmonton, Alberta, in ice and snow. Our plane, about to take off for Fiji with the Queen on board, was delayed. Snow had prevented the crew members from arriving from Vancouver. Eventually, we took off, but an hour or so later, we had to turn back to Edmonton, owing to a hurricane near Fiji.

A large hotel in Edmonton was given only one hour's notice to prepare rooms for forty people in the Queen's entourage—but they managed it. The Royal party arrived at the hotel in the early hours of the morning. It was lovely to find the hotel so warm because it was extremely cold outside.

We had to attend to our Ladies before going to bed, very late. We only had about four hours sleep, as we had to be up for 8 a.m. breakfast, with all our overnight cases packed, ready to take off once more for Fiji."

AUSTRALIA

"'Here come the drones,' we heard the Australian crowds say once. They were referring to the Queen's Household Staff—us, as we rode in cars behind the Queen's car. We laughed. We knew we were far from being drones!"

INDIA

"I met Mrs. Gandhi, who was then a Minister in the Indian Government. She accompanied the Queen everywhere in India. Mrs. Gandhi stayed in the same bungalow as Lady Rose Baring and me in Peshawar. I would see Mrs. Gandhi's manservant bringing out clothes he had pressed for her.

When we were in Calcutta, Lady Rose Baring's room had a wardrobe that was too small to take her dresses. So I had to be resourceful.

I asked a servant to bring me two very large sheets. I placed one of these over the large red screen which shielded the bed in her spacious bedroom. Then I hung my Lady's dresses on hangers on the screen and protected them from dust with the other sheet.

Mrs. Gandhi and a woman on her staff came into the room to see that all was well. They congratulated me on my arrangement for hanging the dresses."

CEYLON (Sri Lanka)

"I liked Ceylon very much. We saw a wonderful elephant procession one night, with all sorts of musicians and dancers. They were parading the Buddha's Tooth.

One ornamented elephant carried the Sacred Tooth and he could only tread on red carpets. So they kept taking up one carpet to put it in front of the other one. What slow progress! Men with dustpans cleared up the elephant droppings."

JAMAICA

"In Jamaica, your Jamaican friends called for me and took me to their home on the sugar estate. There was a banquet for Princess Margaret, at King's House. The bougainvillea is beautiful out there. We saw a large horse-shoe table at the banquet and in the centre there was nothing but bougainvillea. There were all shades, from deep mauve to purple, and pink, gold, apricot, white—like one big cushion, illuminated from below. It was unforgettable."

AFGHANISTAN

"We were up in the Himalayas, where the camels have their own paths up the mountains. People in villages had made arches for the Queen and they had hung Afghan rugs over them to greet her. The Queen's staff had to go around each arch, as the arches were reserved only for the Queen to pass under."

PERSIA (Iran)

"We saw the Crown jewels of Persia the day after the Queen had seen them. She had told all her staff that they *must* go and see them—a sight not to be missed.

The jewels were kept in a spacious strong room under a bank in Tehran. Many detectives were present. There were trays of rubies, emeralds, diamonds—necklaces, tiaras, and rings. We saw the Shah's Peacock Throne too—studded with precious stones—a marvellous sight!"

HOLLAND

"When we were in Holland, Queen Juliana came into the bedroom with Lady Margaret Hay. Lady Margaret said to Queen Juliana, 'This is my Lady's Maid'. I did not curtsey to the Dutch Queen, because I remembered that they don't do that in Holland at all. So, I just gave Queen Juliana a little bow."

DENMARK

"I remember seeing the 'toy' soldiers in Copenhagen, changing the guard to the music of tinny pipes and drums. They were not a patch on our Life Guards!

Epilogue

● ● ● ● ● ● ● ● ● ●

Florence Bramford died on August 8th, 1985, aged 94. A memorial service to celebrate her wonderful life of service was held in St. James' Church, West Malvern. Many old friends came, several from her hometown, Upton-on-Severn.

There were flowers from six of her Ladies in Waiting, and a telegram from Her Majesty the Queen and Princess Margaret, who had known Florence since they were children in wartime.

Her much-loved Lady in Waiting, the Hon. Mary Morrison declared: "A lovely finale for a very special and marvellous person. She was such a dear friend to me. How much she taught me early on in my job! She was always such a support and help, whether it was at home or abroad, keeping one up to the mark in the nicest possible way."

Florence's colleagues wrote too: "I shall always remember Miss Bramford with great affection, especially her sense of fun. A lovely lady."

Others wrote: "She was such a good sport—very popular. We had lots of laughs." "She was so good to me on my first tour, being a novice, pointing out what to do and what not to do, and we became such pals on board *Britannia*."

A very old friend wrote: "I always enjoyed her company. Florence was indeed a Royal subject."

Thank you for reading
*This Was OUR Malvern ~ Worcestershire
& Malvern History Series Book 2
also available on Audible!*

• •

You might also enjoy *From Cottage to Palace ~*
Worcestershire & Malvern History Series Book 1
https://www.amazon.com/dp/B09WB2LQHM
and the audiobook on Audible:
https://www.audible.com/pd/From-Cottage-
to-Palace-Audiobook/B0B3PQTSGZ
and *This Was OUR MALVERN ~*
Worcestershire & Malvern History Series Book 2
https://www.amazon.com/gp/product/B0B1QX1BZ8

For more information about the Worcestershire
& Malvern History Series by Margaret Bramford,
or to sign up for our FREE richardlynttonbooks
(fiction and nonfiction) newsletter, VISIT
this richardlynttonbooks website link:

https://richardlynttonbooks.com/contact/

*If you enjoyed the book, we would very much
appreciate it if you could leave a review on the
platform you used. Thank you so much. God save
Upton, the Pepperpot, and God save King Charles!*

Made in the USA
Middletown, DE
19 October 2022